VOGUE KNITTING

CROCHETED SCARVES

VOGUE KNITTING

CROCHETED
SCARVES

SIXTH&SPRING BOOKS
NEW YORK

SIXTH&SPRING BOOKS
233 Spring Street
New York, New York 10013

Library of Congress Cataloging-in-Publication Data

Vogue knitting crocheted scarves / [book editor, Trisha Malcolm].--1st ed.
p. cm. -- (Vogue knitting on the go!)
ISBN 1-931543-42-9
1. Crocheting--Patterns. 2. Scarves. I. Title: Crochet scarves. II. Malcolm, Trisha,
1960- III. Vogue knitting international. IV. Series.

TT825 .V6235 2004
746.43'40432--dc21   2003054204

Manufactured in China

1 3 5 7 9 10 8 6 4 2

First Edition

TABLE OF CONTENTS

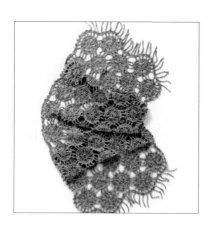

INTRODUCTION

When did you learn how to crochet? Maybe it was at the age of six or seven at Granny's knee. She might have taught you how to sew a blanket-stitched edging around a linen handkerchief. The next step would have been chain loops crocheted from stitch to stitch, followed by a round of fancy scallops, shells or picots.

For some of us, a favorite babysitter might have shown us how to make a simple sweater for a beloved teddy bear. You might have learned how to crochet the classic granny square from a college friend—or finished an afghan before life intervened and took you away from all that contemplative pleasure and pride of accomplishment.

Well, now that you've picked up this first "on-the-go" book of crocheted scarves, you're on your way to re-experiencing all that joy. Whether you're a crochet novice or a veteran who is already well and truly "hooked," you'll be able to find the perfect project in this contemporary collection.

Making a scarf is a wonderful way to re-acquaint yourself with crochet. There's no fussing about perfect fit (who needs more stress?), you can carry it along with you wherever you go and if you have little stashes of leftover yarn, they might just find their home in one of these delightful projects.

Use the yarns listed in the materials as suggestions and then experiment with color and texture to your heart's delight. Since you're not making a whole blanket, splurge on a few balls of luxury or novelty yarn to make an accessory that will brighten your wardrobe.

So, steal a few minutes from your busy life—while riding the bus, waiting for your kids to get out of school or chatting on the phone—to pick up your hook and yarn and **CROCHET ON THE GO!**

THE BASICS

While many crafters consider crochet a family tradition, few may realize that it is a practice that dates back to ancient times. Shepherds were probably the first to crochet, using a hooked stick to turn their spun wool scraps into clothes. By the sixteenth century, Irish nuns were using bone and ivory hooks to create the lace patterns that crocheters still use today. And in the nineteenth century, the aspirational middle classes learned the craft to be like the elite of society, who were educated in such handwork. So crochet became part of popular culture, a practical and artistic craft that anyone could do.

Lately, word is that crochet has made a comeback; history, though, tells us it never really left. People are just exploring new hobbies, rediscovering old skills and expanding their knowledge of handcrafts. Our aim is to encourage and entice a whole spectrum of crocheters, whatever their experience, with this book.

Crochet is accessible and really quite easy to learn. Stitches are formed by pulling loops through other loops or stitches with a hook, creating a simple chain that is used in all patterns. Unlike knitting, there is no balancing act with stitches, shifting them from one needle to another; in crochet, one hand does all the work, and finished fabric lays away from the hook, letting crocheters concentrate on only the newest stitch they need to make. And, unlike other crafts, correcting a mistake is fairly stress free—simply tug on the yarn to easily pull out the stitches you have worked.

If you're not convinced that it's easy to learn to crochet, perhaps the scarves and wraps in this collection will inspire you. They run the gamut from the most basic stitches to more complicated ones, giving experienced crocheters ample selection and offering novices the chance to graduate to more difficult projects as they progress. The beginner scarf styles, such as the Multicolor Mesh Scarf on page 84 and the Mesh Pattern Stole on page 32, often have a simple one-row repeat and work up quickly with a very large hook and bulky weight yarn. Such basic patterns let the yarn take center stage as the star of the style. Meanwhile, the more advanced designs, like the Spoke Motif

Shawl on page 65, do not necessarily have more difficult stitch techniques; rather the instructions, with their series of repeats and pattern layouts, require more concentration to create the perfect piece.

In crochet, finished pieces have unique characteristics. The combination of chains and joining in crochet create a sheer netting, whose airiness can dress up an outfit or just add a dash of style. Other times, the depth of the garment, depending on the chosen yarn, can actually take on a rich three-dimensional appearance. And just as it is easy to learn crochet, it is also easy to finish. Though crocheted pieces often lack stretchability, again, depending on the yarn used, they usually lay flat without further blocking or finishing.

We hope that by now you are convinced to pick up a hook and start to crochet. If not, take a look at the scarves, wraps, shawls and stoles in this dynamic collection; in no time you will be exploring and enjoying the fresh, contemporary styles that have emerged from an ancient tradition.

SCARF STYLES
Scarf
Meant to wrap the neck for warmth, this flat, rectangular piece is usually no more than 12" (30.5cm) wide, and three to 6' (or 6m) in length, but can be any dimension you choose.
Shawl
Rectangular, semicircular or triangular in

CROCHET HOOKS					
U.S.	Metric	U.S.	Metric	U.S.	Metric
14 steel	.60mm	C/2	2.50mm	I/9	5.50mm
12 steel	.75mm	D/3	3.00mm	J/10	6.00mm
10 steel	1.00mm	E/4	3.50mm		6.50mm
6 steel	1.50mm	F/5	4.00mm	K/10.5	7.00mm
5 steel	1.75mm	G/6	4.50mm		
B/1	2.00mm	H/8	5.00mm		

shape, often with a fringed border, the shawl is worn draped around the shoulders. When made in luxurious yarns and patterns, it becomes an elegant evening accessory.

Stole

Wider and longer than a scarf, the stole wraps the torso for warmth. It is a fashionable substitute for a lightweight jacket or sweater. See our Bulky Stole on page 47.

YARN SELECTION

For an exact reproduction of the scarf photographed, use the yarn listed in the materials section of the pattern. We've selected yarns that are readily available in the U.S. and Canada at the time of printing. The Resources list on page 86 provides addresses of yarn distributors. Contact them for the name of a retailer in your area.

YARN SUBSTITUTION

You may wish to substitute yarns. Perhaps a spectacular yarn matches your new coat; maybe you view small-scale projects as a chance to incorporate leftovers from your yarn stash; or it may be that the yarn specified is not available in your area. Scarves allow you to be as creative as you like, but you'll need to crochet to the given gauge to obtain the finished measurements with the substitute yarn. Make pattern adjustments where necessary. Be sure to consider how different yarn types (chenille, mohair, bouclé, etc.) will affect the final appearance of your scarf, and how they will feel against your skin. Also take fiber care into consideration: Some yarns can be machine- or hand-washed; others will require dry cleaning.

To facilitate yarn substitution, Vogue Knitting grades yarn by the standard stitch gauge obtained in single crochet. You'll find a grading number in the "Materials" section of the pattern, immediately following the yarn information. Look for a substitute yarn that falls into the same category. The suggested hook size and gauge on the ball band should be comparable to that on the Standard Yarn Weight chart on page 13.

After you've successfully gauge-swatched a substitute yarn, you'll need to figure out how much of the substitute yarn the project requires. First, find the total length of the original yarn in the pattern (multiply number of balls by yards/meters per ball). Divide this figure by the new yards/meters per ball (listed on the ball band). Round up to the next whole number. The answer is the number of balls required.

Categories of yarn, gauge ranges and recommended needle and hook sizes

Yarn Weight Symbol & Category Names	① Super Fine	② Fine	③ Light	④ Medium	⑤ Bulky	⑥ Super Bulky
Type of Yarns in Category	Sock, Fingering, Baby	Sport, Baby	DK, Light Worsted	Worsted, Afghan, Aran	Chunky, Craft, Rug	Super Bulky, Roving
Knit Gauge Range* in Stockinette Stitch to 4 inches	27–32 sts	23–26 sts	21–24 sts	16–20 sts	12–15 sts	6–11 sts
Recommended Needle in Metric Size Range	2.25–3.25 mm	3.25–3.75 mm	3.75–4.5 mm	4.5–5.5 mm	5.5–8 mm	9–15 mm and larger
Recommended Needle U.S. size range	1 to 3	3 to 5	5 to 7	7 to 9	9 to 11	11 to 19 and larger
Crochet Gauge* Ranges in Single Crochet to 4 inch	21–32 sts	16–20 sts	12–17 sts	11–14 sts	8–11 sts	5–9 sts
Recommended Hook in Metric Size Range	2.25–3.5 mm	3.5–4.5 mm	4.5–5.5 mm	5.5–6.5 mm	6.5–9 mm	9–12 mm and larger
Recommended Hook U.S. Size Range	B-1 to E-4	E-4 to 7	7 to I-9	I-9 to K-10½	K-10½ to M-13	M-13 to P-16 and larger

Beginner
Ideal first project.

Very Easy Very Vogue
Basic stitches, minimal shaping, simple finishing.

Intermediate
For crocheters with some experience. More intricate stitches, shaping and finishing.

Experienced
For crocheters able to work patterns with complicated shaping and finishing.

READING CROCHET INSTRUCTIONS

If you are used to reading knitting instructions, then crochet instructions may seem a little tedious to follow. This is because crochet instructions use more abbreviations and punctuations and fewer words than traditional knitting instructions. Along with the separation of stitches and use of brackets, parentheses, commas and other punctuation, there are numerous repetitions going on within a single row or round. Therefore, you must pay closer attention to reading instructions while you crochet. Here are a few explanations of the more common terminology used in this book.

Use of Parentheses ( )

Sometimes parentheses will be used to indicate the stitches that will be worked all into one stitch such as "in next st work ( )" or "( ) in next st."

First st, Next st

The beginning stitch of every row is referred to as the "first st." When counting the turning chain (t-ch) as one stitch, the row or round will begin by stating to work into the next st (that is, skip the first st or space or whatever is designated in the pattern).

Stitch Counts

Sometimes the turning chain that is worked at the end (or beginning) of a row or a round will be referred to as 1 stitch and then is counted in the stitch count. When the t-ch is counted as 1 stitch, you will work into the next stitch, thus skipping the first stitch of the row or round. When the t-ch is not counted as a stitch, work into the first stitch.

Stitches Described

Sometimes the stitches are described as sc, dc, tr, ch-2 loop, 2-dc group, etc. and sometimes—such as in a mesh pattern of sc, ch 1—each sc and each ch 1 will be referred to as a st.

Back Loop

Along the top of each crochet stitch or chain there are two loops. The loop furthest away from you is the "back loop."

Front Loop

Along the top of each crochet stitch or chain there are two loops. The loop closest to you is the "front loop."

Joining New Colors

When joining new colors in crochet, whether at the beginning of a row or while working across, always work the stitch in the old color to the last 2 loops, then draw the new color through the 2 loops and continue with the new color.

Working Over Ends

Crochet has a unique flat top along each row that is perfect for laying the old color across and working over the ends for several stitches. This will alleviate the cutting and weaving in of ends later.

Form a Ring

When a pattern is worked in the round, as

in a square or medallion, the beginning chains are usually closed into a ring by working a slip stitch into the first chain. Then on the first round, stitches are usually worked into the ring and less often into each chain.

BLOCKING

Blocking crochet is usually not necessary. However, in those cases when you do need to smooth out the fabric, choose a blocking method according to the yarn care label and, when in doubt, test your gauge swatch. Note that some yarns, such as chenilles and ribbons, do not benefit from blocking.

Wet Block Method

Using rustproof pins, pin scarf to measurements on a flat surface and lightly dampen using a spray bottle. Allow to dry before removing pins.

Steam Block Method

Pin scarf to measurements with wrong side of the fabric facing up. Steam lightly, holding the iron 2"/5cm above the work. Do not press the iron onto the piece, as it will flatten the stitches.

CARE

Refer to the yarn label for the recommended cleaning method. Many of the scarves in the book can be washed by hand (or in the machine on a gentle or wool cycle) in lukewarm water with a mild detergent. Do not agitate, and don't soak for more than 10 minutes. Rinse gently with tepid water, then fold in a towel and gently press the water out. Lay flat to dry, away from excessive heat and light.

FRINGE

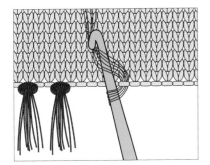

SIMPLE FRINGE: Cut yarn twice desired length plus extra for knotting. On wrong side, insert hook from front to back through piece and over folded yarn. Pull yarn through. Draw ends through and tighten. Trim yarn.

KNOTTED FRINGE: After working a simple fringe (it should be longer to allow for extra knotting), take one half of the strands from each fringe and knot them with half the strands from the neighboring fringe.

CHAIN

1 *Pass the yarn over the hook and catch it with the hook.*

2 *Draw the yarn through the loop on the hook.*

3 *Repeat steps 1 and 2 to make a chain.*

SINGLE CROCHET

1 *Insert the hook through top two loops of a stitch. Pass the yarn over the hook and draw up a loop—two loops on hook.*

2 *Pass the yarn over the hook and draw through both loops on hook.*

3 *Continue in the same way, inserting the hook into each stitch.*

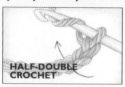

HALF-DOUBLE CROCHET

1 *Pass the yarn over the hook. Insert the hook through the top two loops of a stitch.*

2 *Pass the yarn over the hook and draw up a loop—three loops on hook. Pass the yarn over the hook.*

3 *Draw through all three loops on hook.*

DOUBLE CROCHET

1 *Pass the yarn over the hook. Insert the hook through the top two loops of a stitch.*

2 *Pass the yarn over the hook and draw up a loop—three loops on hook.*

SLIP STITCH

Insert the crochet hook into a stitch, catch the yarn and pull up a loop. Draw the loop through the loop on the hook.

3 *Pass the yarn over the hook and draw it through the first two loops on the hook, pass the yarn over the hook and draw through the remaining two loops. Continue in the same way, inserting the hook into each stitch.*

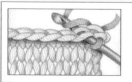

approx approximately

beg begin(ning)

CC contrast color

ch chain(s)

cm centimeter(s)

cont continue(ing)

dc double crochet (UK: tr-treble)

dec decrease(ing)–Reduce the stitches in a row (work stitches together or skip the stitches).

foll follow(s)(ing)

g gram(s)

hdc half double crochet (UK: htr-half treble)

inc increase(ing)–Add stitches in a row (work extra stitches into a stitch or between the stitches).

LH left-hand

lp(s) loop(s)

m meter(s)

MC main color

mm millimeter(s)

oz ounce(s)

pat(s) pattern

pm place markers–Place or attach a loop of contrast yarn or purchased stitch marker as indicated.

rem remain(s)(ing)

rep repeat

rnd(s) round(s)

RH right-hand

RS right side(s)

sc single crochet (UK: dc-double crochet)

sk skip

sl st slip stitch (UK: single crochet)

sp(s) space(s)

st(s) stitch(es)

t-ch turning chain

tog together

tr treble (UK: tr tr-triple treble)

WS wrong side(s)

work even Continue in pattern without increasing or decreasing. (UK: work straight)

yd yard(s)

yo yarn over–wrap the yarn around the hook (UK: yrh)

* = repeat directions following * as many times as indicated.

[ ] = Repeat directions inside brackets as many times as indicated.

■■■■

Work two scallop-edged strips in an open work scale pattern to create this delicate mohair scarf, boasting festoons of flowers. Large picot-edged scallops finish off the ends of this scarf designed by Michelle Woodford.

FINISHED MEASUREMENTS

▨ Approx 12"/30.5cm wide x 56"/142cm long

MATERIALS

▨ 4 .88oz/25g balls (each approx 269yd/242m) of Filatura di Crosa/Tahki•Stacy Charles, Inc. *Baby Kid Extra* (mohair/nylon) in #461 raspberry (▨)
▨ Size J/10 (6mm) crochet hook *or size to obtain gauge*

GAUGE

15 dc and 8 dc rows to 4"/10cm over dc pat using 2 strands of yarn and size J/10 (6mm) crochet hook.
Take time to check gauge.

Notes

1 Work with 2 strands of yarn held tog throughout.

2 Scarf is constructed by first working one scallop edge, then continuing with the openwork scale pat for one strip. The second strip is worked in the same way, then the two strips are joined tog by an inset of flowers that run through the center.

SCARF

SCALLOP EDGE

With 2 strands of yarn held tog, ch 6. Join with a sl st to first ch to form ring.

Rnd 1 Ch 3 (counts as 1 dc), work 8 dc in ring—9 dc total. Arrange the 9 dc so that they are around half the ring only. The rest of the scallop edge will be worked back and forth in rows to form the scallop edge in the semicircle pattern (as shown in photo). Turn.

Row 2 Ch 4 (counts as 1 dc and ch-1), skip first dc, *1 dc in next dc, ch 1; rep from *, end 1 dc in last dc. There are 9 dc and 8 ch-1 sps. Turn.

Row 3 Ch 3, 2 dc in first ch-1 sp, *3 dc in next ch-1 sp; rep from * to end—24 dc. Turn.

Row 4 Ch 6 (counts as 1 dc and ch-3), work 1 dc in 3rd dc, *ch 3, skip 2 dc, 1 dc in next dc; rep from * to end. There are 9 dc and 8 ch-3 sps. Turn.

Row 5 Ch 3 (counts as 1 dc), *work 3 dc in ch-3 sp, 1 dc in next dc; rep from * to end—33 dc. Turn.

Row 6 Ch 4 (counts as 1 dc and ch-1), 1 dc in 3rd dc, *ch 1, skip 1 dc, 1 dc in next dc; rep from * to end. Turn.

Row 7 Ch 3 (counts as 1 dc), 2 dc in first ch-1 sp, *3 dc in next ch-1 sp; rep from * to end—48 dc. Turn.

Row 8 Ch 3 (counts as 1 dc), *1 dc in each of next 7 dc, 2 dc in next dc; rep from * ending with 7 dc in last 7 dc—53 dc. Turn.

Row 9 Ch 3 (counts as 1 dc), 1 dc in next dc, then in next st work *dc picot* as foll: 1 dc, ch 4, work 1 sl st into top of dc just worked, *1 dc in each of next 6 dc, work dc picot in next st; rep from *, end with 1 dc in last st. Do *not* turn.

BEG OPENWORK SCALE PATTERN

Working across the straight edge of the scallop edge just made work as foll:

Row 10 Ch 3 (counts as 1 dc), *work 2 dc around horizontal dc st*; rep between *'s 8 times more, work 5 dc in center loop, rep between *'s 9 times more, end with 1 dc in last st—43 dc. Turn.

Row 11 Ch 3 (counts as 1 dc), 1 dc in each of next 2 sts, *skip 2 sts, 5 dc in next st, (on subsequent rows, this will be a ch-3 sp), skip 2 sts, 1 dc in each of next 3 sts; rep from * to end. Turn.

Row 12 Ch 3 (counts as 1 dc), 1 dc in each of next 2 sts, *2 dc in space (space is formed between the 3 dc and 5 dc of previous row), ch 3, 2 dc in space, 1 dc in each of next 3 sts; rep from * to end. Turn. Rep rows 11 and 12 for a total of 19 times more. Rep row 11 once more. Cut yarn. Work a second scallop and openwork scale pat strip in same way.

CENTER FLORAL STRIP

With 2 strands of yarn held tog, ch 45.

Row 1 Work 1 dc in 4th ch from hook, skip 3 ch, then in next ch work *tr tr bobble* as foll: *yo hook twice, insert hook into ch, draw lp through, yo, draw through 2 lps, yo and through 2 lps again (2 lps rem on hook)*, then into same ch, rep between *'s twice, yo and draw lp through rem 4 lps on hook, [ch 3, work tr tr bobble in same ch] twice, skip 3 ch, work 1 dc in next ch, skip 3 ch; rep from * 4 times more, end last rep with 1 dc in each of last 2 ch. Turn.

Row 2 Ch 3 (counts as 1 dc), 1 dc in next st, *ch 3, 1 sc in space between tr tr bobble, ch 3, 1 dc in space between tr tr bobble, ch 3, 1 dc in top of 2 lps of dc on previous row; rep from * 4 times more, ending with 1 dc in last st. Fasten off. Turn floral strip to work from opposite side of beg ch and work rows 1 and 2 into the opposite side of the ch, completing flowers.

FINISHING

Block lightly to measurements. Pin or baste center floral strip to first openwork scale strips. Join tog as foll: *work 1 sc in scarf edge, ch 2, 1 sc in corresponding center floral edge, ch 2, skip 1 st; rep from * until strip is joined. Work 2nd openwork scale strip joining in same way.

■ ■ ■ ■ ▢

A graphic combination of black and white enhances this jagged stripe scarf, worked in a simple single crochet and chain stitch. Alternating hearts are attached with tassel fringe at each end. Designed by Gayle Bunn.

FINISHED MEASUREMENTS
■ 6½"/16.5cm wide x 66"/168cm long, excluding heart fringe

MATERIALS
■ 2 3½oz/100g balls (each approx 223yd/204m) of Patons® *Classic Merino Wool* (wool) each in #226 black (A) and #201 white (B) 🄴
■ One each sizes G/6 (4.5mm) and I/9 (5.5mm) crochet hooks *or size to obtain gauge*

GAUGE
18 sts and 19 rows to 4"/10cm over stripe pat st using larger hook.
Take time to check gauge.

Note
1 Each sc and ch 1 is counted as 1 st.
2 When changing colors, work to last 2 loops of working color, draw new color through these last 2 loops and beg working with new color.

SCARF
With larger hook and A, loosely chain 298.
Row 1 (RS) Work 1 sc in 2nd ch from hook, *ch 1, skip 1 ch, 1 sc in next ch; rep from * to end, turn—297 sts.

Row 2 With A, ch 1, 1 sc in first sc, *1 sc in next ch-1 sp, ch 1, skip next sc; rep from * to last 2 sts, 1 sc in last ch-1 sp, 1 sc in last sc, joining B at end, turn.

Row 3 With B, ch 1, 1 sc in first sc, *ch 1, skip next sc, 1 sc in next ch-1 sp; rep from * to last 2 sts, ch 1, skip next st, 1 sc in last sc, turn.

Row 4 With B, rep row 2, joining A at end, turn.

Row 5 With A, rep row 3.

Row 6 With A, rep row 2.

Rep rows 3-6 for pat 6 times more. Fasten off.

HEART A
(make 4)
With smaller hook and A, ch 2.
Rnd 1 Work 6 sc in 2nd ch from hook, join with sl st to first sc.

Rnd 2 Ch 1, 2 sc in each of the next 3 sc, 3 sc in next sc, 2 sc in each of the next 2 sc—13 sc. Do *not* join, turn. Work rem of heart in rows.

Row 3 Working around the first sc, work 1 dc in center sp of the first rnd, 1 sc in each of next 2 sc, 1 sl st in each of next 3 sc, 3 sc in next sc, 1 sl st in each of next 3 sc, 1 sc in each of next 2 sc, 1 dc around the last sc and into center sp of the first rnd, joining B at end, turn.

Row 4 With B, ch 1, sc in first dc, 1 sc in each of next 2 sc, 1 sc in each of next 3 sl sts, 1 sc in next sc, 3 sc in next sc, 1 sc in next sc, 1 sc in next 3 sl sts, 1 sc in each of next 2 sc, 1 sc in last dc, 2 sc down side of same dc, sc3tog (by drawing up a lp in each of next 3 sc, yo, and through all loops on hook) over inner curve of heart, 2 sc up side of next dc, join with sl st to first sc. Fasten off.

HEART B
(make 4)
Work as for heart A, substituting color A for B and B for A.

FINISHING
Alternating A and B hearts, sew hearts to scarf ends tacking through the 2 top corners of each heart and tacking hearts tog through one st at each side edge of heart (see photo).

FRINGE
Cut 14"/36cm lengths of A, having 6 lengths for each fringe. Pull fringe through each of the 3 heart points at each end of scarf.

MOHAIR RIPPLE SCARF
New wave

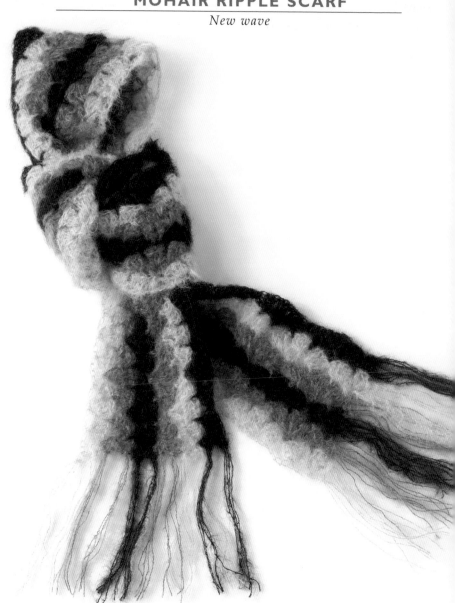

■■■■▢

Twelve rows is all it takes to make this cluster pattern scarf designed by Katherine Fedewa. Crochet this scarf lengthwise in autumn-friendly earth-tone hues.

FINISHED MEASUREMENTS
Approx 5"/12.5cm wide x 65"/165cm long (excluding fringe)

MATERIALS
1 .88oz/25g ball (each approx 109yd/100m) of Le Fibre Nobili/ Plymouth Yarns *Imperiale* (mohair/nylon) each in #4123 lt green (A), #4122 green (B) and #4119 brown (C) (**3**)
Size I/9 (5.5mm) crochet hook *or size to obtain gauge*

GAUGE
One 9-dc scallop to 2¾"/7cm and 6 rows to 2½"/6.5cm over scallop pat st using size I/9 (5.5mm) crochet hook.
Take time to check gauge.

SCALLOP PATTERN STITCH
Chain a multiple of 11 ch plus 10.
Row 1 Work 1 dc in 4th ch from hook, ch 1, skip 2 ch, 1 sc in next ch, *ch 5, skip 4 ch, 1 sc in next ch, ch 1, skip 2 ch, in next ch work (1 dc, ch 1, 1 dc), ch 1, skip 2 ch, 1 sc in next ch; rep from *, end ch 2, skip 2 ch, 1 dc in last ch. Ch 1, turn.
Row 2 Work 1 sc in first dc, skip ch-2 sp, *work 3 dc in next each of next 3 ch 1-sps, 1 sc in next ch-5 sp; rep from *, end 3 dc in last ch-1 sp, 2 dc in 3rd ch of t-ch. Ch 4, turn.

Row 3 Work 1 sc in between 2nd and 3rd dc, *ch 1, in next sc work (1 dc, ch 1, 1 dc), ch 1, 1 sc in between next 3rd and 4th dc, ch 5, 1 sc in between next 3rd and 4th dc; rep from *, end ch 1, 2 dc in last sc, skip t-ch. Ch 3, turn.
Row 4 Work 1 dc in first dc, 3 dc in ch-1 sp, *1 sc in ch-5 sp, work 3 dc in each of next 3 ch-1 sps; rep from *, end 1 sc in t-ch sp. Ch 3, turn.
Row 5 Work 1 dc in first sc, ch 1, *1 sc in between next 3rd and 4th dc, ch 5, 1 sc in between next 3rd and 4th dc, ch 1, in next sc work (1 dc, ch 1, 1 dc), ch 1; rep from *, end 1 sc in between 3rd and 4th dc, ch 2, 1 dc in 3rd ch of t-ch. Ch 1, turn.
Rep rows 2-5 for scallop pattern st.

SCARF
With A, ch 263.
Note Leave a 6"/15cm length of each color when cutting and beg with a new color. With A, work rows 1 and 2 of pat st. Work B, work rows 3 and 4 of pat st. With C, work rows 5 and 2 of pat st. With B, work rows 3 and 4 of pat st. With A, work rows 5 and 2 of pat st. With C, work rows 3 and 4 of pat st. Fasten off.

FINISHING
Block scarf lightly to measurements.

FRINGE
Cut 16 strands 11"/28cm long of each of the 3 colors, A, B and C. Fold each fringe in half and pull through where 6"/15cm length ends of scarf were left. Trim ends evenly.

FISHNET SHAWL

Sheer intensity

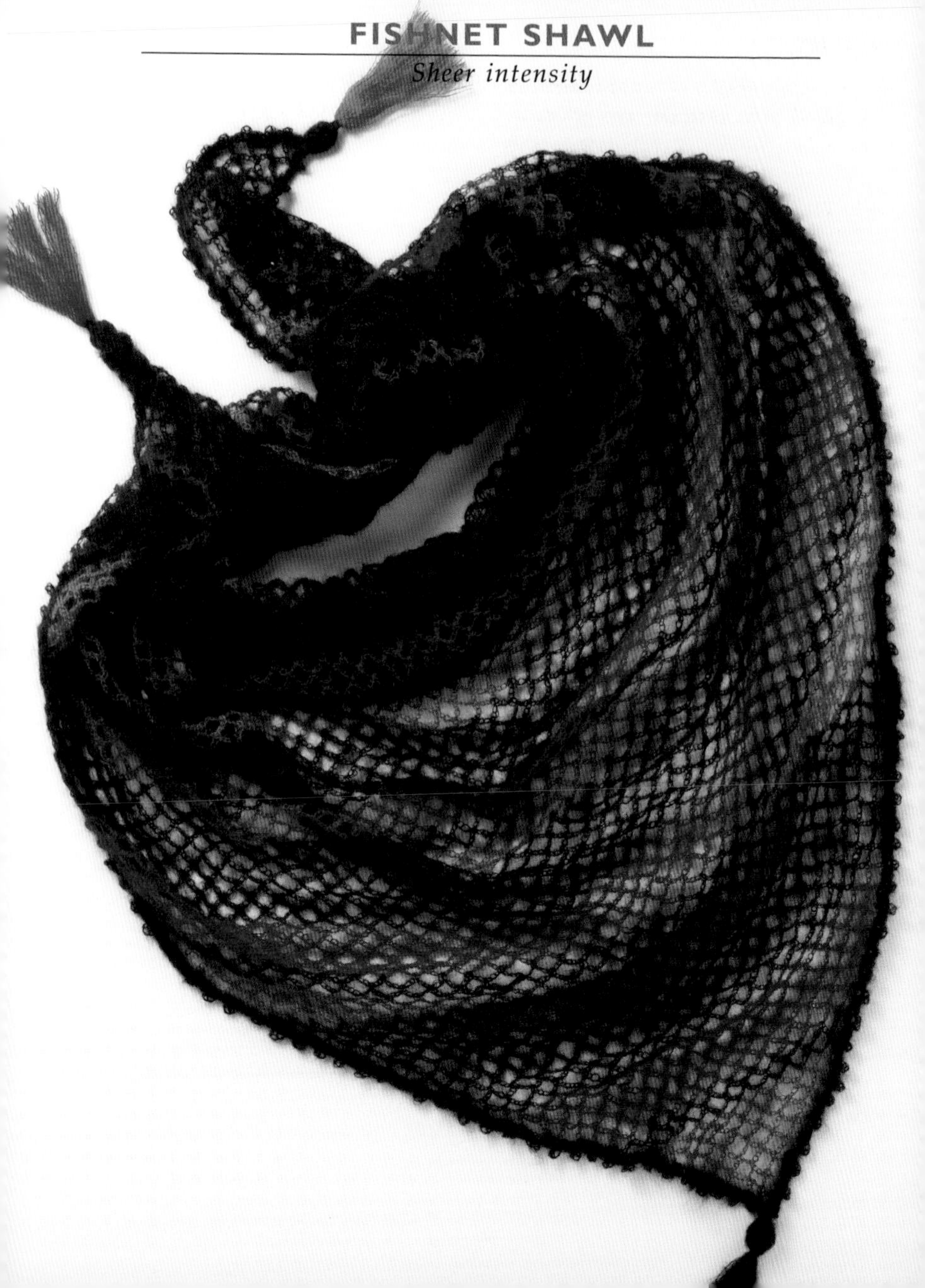

■■■■▭

A gossamer weight of kid mohair and silk blend yarn provides the whisper-soft background for this triangular shawl. Trimmed with corner tassels, it is crocheted in an airy fishnet chain pattern stitch. Designed by Sasha Kagan.

FINISHED MEASUREMENTS
■ Approx 74"/188cm at straight edge along top of triangle and 48"/122cm at center depth of triangle

MATERIALS
■ 2 .88oz/25g balls (each approx 227yd/210m) of Rowan Yarn *Kid Silk Haze* (mohair/silk) in #599 black (A) (🔟)
■ 1 ball each in #595 burgundy (B), #606 hot pink (C) and #596 orange (D)
■ Size D/3 (3mm) crochet hook *or size to obtain gauge*
■ Tapestry needle

GAUGE
5 chain-5 loops and 9 rows to 4"/10cm over fishnet chain pat using size D/3 (3mm) crochet hook.
Take time to check gauge.

SHAWL

With black (A), ch 405 loosely.
Row 1 Work 1 sl st in 5th ch from hook, *ch 5, skip 3 ch, 1 sl st in next ch; rep from * to end—101 ch-5 loops. Turn.
Row 2 Sl st into first 3 ch of ch-5 loop, *ch 5, 1 sl st into next ch-5 loop; rep from * to end. One ch-5 loop has been decreased at beg of row. Rep row 2 for fishnet chain pat throughout working in the foll color sequence:
Rows 3-5 Use black (A).
Rows 6 and 7 Use burgundy (B).
Rows 8 and 9 Use black (A).
Rows 10 and 11 Use hot pink (C).
Rows 12 and 13 Use black (A).
Rows 14 and 15 Use orange (D).
Rows 16 and 17 Use black (A).
Rows 18-20 Use burgundy (B).
Rows 21 and 22 Use black (A).
Rows 23-25 Use hot pink (C).
Rows 26 and 27 Use black (A).
Rows 28-30 Use orange (D).
Rows 31 and 32 Use black (A).
Rows 33-36 Use burgundy (B).
Rows 37 and 38 Use black (A).
Rows 39-42 Use hot pink (C).
Rows 43 and 44 Use black (A).
Rows 45-48 Use orange (D).
Rows 49 and 50 Use black (A).
Rows 51-55 Use burgundy (B).
Rows 56 and 57 Use black (A).
Rows 58-62 Use hot pink (C).
Rows 63 and 64 Use black (A).
Rows 65-71 Use orange (D).
Rows 72 and 73 Use black (A).
Rows 74-80 Use burgundy (B).
Rows 81 and 82 Use black (A).
Rows 83-89 Use hot pink (C).
Rows 90 and 91 Use black (A).
Rows 92-99 Use orange (D).
Rows 100 and 101 Use black (A)—one ch-5 loop remains. Cut yarn.

FINISHING

With black (A), join with a sl st at top right hand corner of foundation ch.

Rnd 1 Work 5 hdc in first ch-3 sp, then work 3 hdc in each ch-3 sp along top of shawl to last sp, work 5 hdc in this sp, work 3 hdc in side of each ch-5 loop to bottom point of triangle, work 5 hdc in point of triangle, work 3 hdc in side of each ch-5 loop to top of shawl, join with a sl st to first hdc.

Rnd 2 Ch 1, work 1 sc in next 2 hdc, (sc, ch 2 and sc) in center hdc for corner, *1 sc in next 2 hdc, then work 1 sc in next hdc, ch 3 (for picot), 1 sc in same hdc, 1 sc in each of next 2 hdc; rep from * to top corner, work corner as at beg, rep from * to bottom point, work corner as at beg, rep from * to end. Join and fasten off.

TASSELS

Make 3, using black (A) for crochet base and 1 each burgundy (B), hot pink (C) and orange (D) for tassel strands.

TASSEL STRANDS

Cut one 4½"/11.5cm piece of cardboard. Wind yarn several times around cardboard. Cut yarn. Thread tapestry needle with corresponding color through uncut end of loops and pull through and tighten. Cut other end of loops. Fasten tassel securely at top and pull end into tassel ends.

CROCHET BASE (MAKE 3)

With black (A), ch 3, leaving a long end. Join with a sl st to first ch to form ring.

Rnd 1 Ch 1, work 6 sc into ring. Join with a sl st to first sc.

Rnd 2 Ch 1, *1 sc in next st, 2 sc in next st; rep from * around—9 sc. Join with a sl st to first sc.

Rnd 3 Ch 1, work 1 sc in each sc around. Join with a sl st to first sc.

Rnd 4 Rep rnd 2, end sc in last st—13 sc. Join with a sl st to first sc.

Rnds 5-7 Rep rnd 3.

Join tassel strands to rnd 7 of crochet base. Wind black (A) several times around tassel to hold firmly in place. Join 3 tassels to points of the triangle as in photo.

FUN FUR SCARF
Strip teaser

■■■▢

Sumptuous strips of fur-like yarn are held together with chains worked in a light-weight wool. Whimsical fur-trimmed tails accentuate both ends. Designed by Mari Lynn Patrick.

FINISHED MEASUREMENTS
■ Approx 7½"/19cm x 74"/188cm, excluding chain trim

MATERIALS
■ 4 1¾oz/50g balls (each approx 86yd/80m) of GGH/Muench Yarns *Esprit* (polyamid) in #26 lt green (A) (5)
■ 3 1¾oz/50g balls (each approx 119yd/110m) of GGH/Muench Yarns *Maxima* (wool) in #13 lt green (B) (3)
■ One each sizes I/9 (5.5mm) and J/10 (6mm) crochet hooks *or size to obtain gauge*

GAUGE
11 hdc to 4"/10cm and 2 hdc rows to 1¼"/3cm using A and size J/10 (6mm) hook. *Take time to check gauge.*

Note Scarf is worked lengthwise. Be sure to chain *loosely* and to work pattern very loosely, especially when working with the lighter weight Maxima (B) Yarn.

SCARF
With size J/10 (6mm) hook and A, chain 200.

Row 1 (RS) With A, [yo and pull up a lp in 2nd ch from hook, yo and through 2 lps on hook] twice, yo and through all 3 lps for 1 puff st at the edge, work 1 hdc in each ch to last st, work 1 puff st in last st. Cut A. Rejoin A at beg to work next row from RS.

Row 2 (RS) Join A, ch 3, work 1 puff st in first st, work 1 hdc in each hdc to last st, work 1 puff st in last st, pulling B through last 2 lps on hook. Ch 1, turn.

Row 3 (WS) With B, working very loosely, work 1 sc in each hdc to end. Ch 1, turn.

Row 4 (RS) With B, working very loosely, work 1 sc in first sc, *ch 3, skip 3 sc, work 1 sc in next sc; rep from *, end 1 sc in last sc. Ch 1, turn.

Row 5 (WS) With B, working very loosely, work 1 sc in first 2 sc, *3 sc in ch-3 sp, 1 sc in next sc; rep from * to end, pulling A through last 2 lps on hook. Ch 3, turn.

Row 6 (RS) With A, work 1 puff st in first st, work 1 hdc in each st to last st, work 1 puff st in last st. Cut A. Rejoin A at beg to work next row from RS.

Rep rows 2-6 three times more.

Next row (RS) *Work 1 hdc in each of next 7 hdc, yo and draw up a lp in next 2 sc, yo and through all lps on hook to dec 1 hdc; rep from * to last 2 hdc, 1 hdc in each of last 2 hdc, ch 1, turn.

Last row Work 1 sl st in each st across (to keep edge as firm as the beg chain edge). Fasten off.

FINISHING
Do not block or press.

CHAIN TAILS
(make 10)
With size I/9 (5.5mm) hook and A, ch 3, join with sl st to first ch to form ring.
Rnd 1 Work 4 sc in ring.
Rnd 2 Work 1 sc in each sc around. Do *not* join.
Rnd 3 Rep rnd 2.
Rnd 4 *Pull up a lp in next 2 sc, yo and through 3 loops on hook; rep from * once.
Rnd 5 Rep from * of rnd 4 once, draw 2 strands B through last 2 loops on hook. With 2 strands B, ch 10. Pull through last lp of chain to attach to center of one strip in A. Fasten securely in place. Fasten in all ends securely inside of tail and to WS of scarf. Work all chain tails in same way.

The tubular knit tape yarn used in this stole design has been dyed in multicolor stripes giving it a deep fabric body. Designed by Norah Gaughan, this stole is crocheted in a simple double crochet mesh pattern.

FINISHED MEASUREMENTS
◼ Approx 21"/53cm x 66"/168cm

MATERIALS
◼ 13 1¾oz/50g balls (each approx 66yd/60m) of Artful Yarns/JCA, Inc. *Vaudeville* (wool) in #7 blue multicolor ⑥
◼ Size M/13 (9mm) crochet hook *or size to obtain gauge*

GAUGE
11 sts to 4"/10cm and 11 mesh pat rows to 8"/20cm over mesh pat st using size M/13 (9mm) crochet hook.
Take time to check gauge.

Note (on gauge) When an extra bulky weight of yarn is used in combination with this very large hook size, it is not recommended to change hook sizes to fit the gauge. Therefore, try to work the gauge swatch with a looser or tighter tension to achieve the look of the fabric in this style.

Note (on stitches) The "stitches" that are referred to in the gauge represent either dc or ch for easier counting for gauge. One dc plus a ch-1 will also be referred to in the instructions as 1 mesh space.

Note (on ends) You may want to crochet over the ends while working to avoid weaving in later.

MESH PATTERN STITCH
Chain a multiple of 2 ch plus 1 extra ch.
Row 1 Work 1 dc in 3rd ch from hook, *ch 1, skip 1 ch, 1 dc in next ch; rep from * to end. Ch 3, turn.
Row 2 Work 1 dc in first ch-1 sp, *ch 1, 1 dc in next ch-1 sp; rep from * to end.
Rep row 2 for mesh pat st. Pattern is reversible.

STOLE
Chain 61. Work even in mesh pat st on 30 mesh spaces until piece measures approx 66"/168cm from beg. Fasten off.

FINISHING
Do *not* block or flatten piece. If necessary, weave in all ends over several stitches and cut carefully.

Knots landing

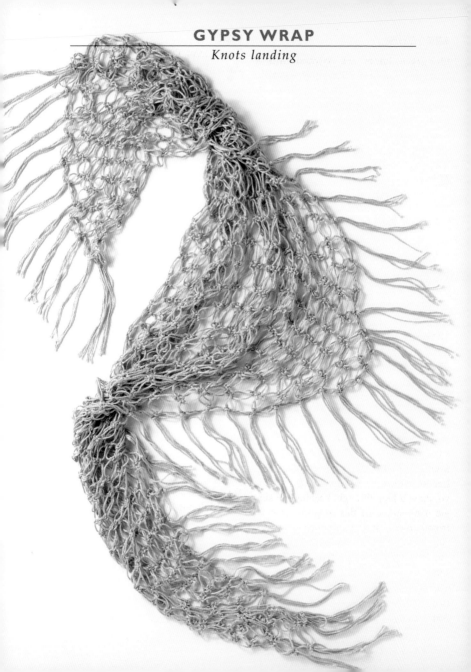

■■■■

Elongated knots are formed into a four-loop diamond shape in this totally breezy triangular wrap. Designed in a silky cotton and tencel blend yarn by Katherine Fedewa.

FINISHED MEASUREMENTS
■ Approx 56"/142cm wide along top and 31"/78.5cm deep, excluding fringe.

MATERIALS
■ 3 1¾oz/50g balls (each approx 108yd/99m) of Classic Elite Yarn *Premiere* (cotton/Tencel) in #5235 lime (1)
■ Size I/9 (5.5mm) crochet hook *or size to obtain gauge*

GAUGE
Each 4-loop diamond shape to approx 1¾"/4.5cm x 1¾"/4.5cm using size I/9 (5.5mm) crochet hook.
Take time to check gauge.

Note The length of the loops for this pattern are given in centimeters (cm) only to reflect a more accurate length.

STITCH GLOSSARY
Solomon's knot (SK)
Lengthen loop on hook to length required, yo, draw a loop through, keeping the single back strand of this long ch separate from 2 front strands, insert hook under this single back strand, yo, draw loop through, yo, draw through both loops on hook.

ESK
These form the base "chain" and are only two-thirds the length of MSK's—approx 2cm long.

MSK
These form the main fabric and are 1½ times as long as ESK's—approx 3cm long.

WRAP
Base chain Ch 2, 1 sc in 2nd ch from hook, 4 ESK, 1 MSK.
Row 1 1 sc in sc between 3rd and 4th loops (lengthened Solomon Loops) from hook, 2 MSK, skip 2 loops, 1 sc in next sc (first sc of base chain), turn. **Row 2** 3 MSK, 1 sc in sc between 4th and 5th loops from hook (for a 4-loop diamond), 2 MSK, skip 2 loops, 1 sc in next sc (for 2nd 4-loop diamond), turn—two 4-loop diamonds. **Row 3** 3 MSK, 1 sc in sc between 4th and 5th loops from hook, 2 MSK, skip 2 loops, 1 sc in next sc, 2 MSK, insert hook in sc between 3rd and 4th loops from hook, yo, draw loop through, lengthen to 3cm, yo, draw through long loop only, keeping the single back strand of this long st separate from the 2 front strands, insert the hook under this single back strand, yo, draw a loop through, yo, draw through 3 loops on hook—three 4-loop diamonds. Rep row 3 for 25 more times, adding one 4-loop diamond on each row—28 4-loop diamonds total. **Row 29** 2 MSK, 1 sc in sc between 3rd and 4th loops from hook *1 MSK, skip 2 loops, 1 sc in next sc; rep from *, end 2 MSK, 1 sc in sc between 3rd and 4th loops from hook. Fasten off.

FINISHING
Fringe
Cut 11"/28cm strands of yarn. Using 2 strands for each fringe, attach 1 fringe to each sc knot along the lower 2 edges of the triangular wrap. Trim ends.

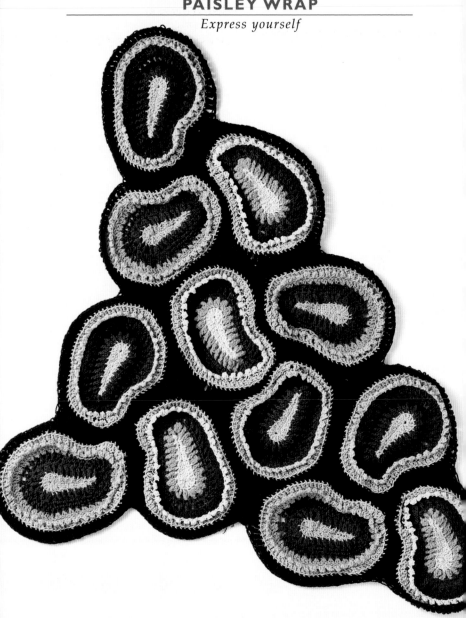

■ ■ ■ ▶

Floating paisley shapes are joined with a unique interlocking - shaped edge in this innovative triangular paisley neck scarf. It's designed by Teva Durham in a stretchy nylon and cotton crepe textured yarn.

FINISHED MEASUREMENTS

▢ Approx 33"/84cm wide along top of triangle and 22"/56cm deep

MATERIALS

▢ 1 1¾oz/50g skein (each approx 190yd/174m) each of Knit One Crochet Too *Frosting* (cotton/nylon) in #212 burgundy (MC) and #918 pale grey (K) (**2**)
▢ One half or less skein each of #411 apricot (A), #510 pale green (B), #699 pale blue (C), #800 brown (D), #823 rust (E), #423 yellow (F), #631 blue (G) and #559 grey (H)
▢ Small amount #248 rose (I) and #645 navy (J)
▢ Size D/3 (3mm) crochet hook *or size to obtain gauge*

GAUGE

20 sts and 8 rows to 4"/10cm over dc using size D/3 (3mm) crochet hook.
Take time to check gauge.

Note The stretch in this yarn facilitates the piecing together of irregular shapes, so if substituting yarn, it is best to use something with stretch.

Paisley A (make 4)

With A, chain 16.

Rnd 1 Sl st in each of first 5 ch, sc in next 4 ch, hdc in next 3 ch, dc in next 2 ch, dc 10 times into last ch, do not turn work, but cont along opposite side of foundation chain with dc in next 2 ch, hdc in next 3 ch, sc in next 4 ch, sl st in next 5 ch, sl st in first sl st of rnd. Fasten off.

Rnd 2 Join color D in st that joined foundation rnd, ch 3, working through *back* loops of sts only, work 2 dc in same st, remove hook from loop, insert hook into the space between ch and first dc, pull dropped loop through, ch 1, to form a popcorn (make subsequent popcorns by 3 dc in same st, remove hook from loop, insert hook into the space between last popcorn and first dc, pull dropped loop through ch 1). After first popcorn at beg of rnd, work a popcorn in every other st 8 times, work popcorn in every st 8 times, work popcorn in every other st 7 times, work popcorn into ch at beg of rnd, ch 1, sl st into top of ch of first popcorn. Fasten off.

Rnd 3 Join color E in first space of rnd, sc in first space, ch 1, (sc, ch 1, sc) into next space, working in the spaces between each st of last rnd, [ch 1, sc] 6 times, [ch 1, sc, ch 1, sc] 9 times, [ch 1, sc] 8 times, ch 1, sc in the space created by first ch-1 of rnd, ch 1, sl st in first sc of rnd. Fasten off.

Rnd 4 Join color I in first space, ch 3, dc in same space, ch 1, (tr, ch 1) 3 times in next space, working into spaces between sts of last rnd, ch 1, dc, ch 1, hdc, ch 1, sc, sl st, ch 1, sc, [ch 1, dc] 29 times, ch 1, join rnd with sl st to 3rd chain at beg of rnd. Fasten off.

Rnd 5 Join color F in first space of rnd, ch 2, dc into same space, 2 dc in next space, (tr 3 times, dc) in next space, (hdc, sc) in next space, sl st in next 6 spaces, sc in next space, (hdc, dc) in next space, 2 dc in next space, 3 dc in next space, [2 dc in next space] 3 times, [3 dc in next space] 5 times, [2 dc in next space] 5 times, dc in next space, 2 hdc in each of the next spaces to end of rnd. Join rnd with sl st into 2nd ch of rnd. Fasten off.

Rnd 6 Join color A to the st that joined last rnd, working through the *back* loops of sts only, *ch 3, sl st in first ch (for a picot), skip 1 st, sl st into next st; rep from * to end of rnd, sl st in first ch of rnd. Fasten off.

Paisley B (make 4)

Work as for Paisley A, using color B for foundation rnd, color H for rnd 2, color J for rnd 3, color G for rnd 4, color E for rnd 5, color B for rnd 6.

Paisley C (make 4)

Work as for Paisley A, using color C for foundation rnd, color F for rnd 2, color D for rnd 3, color H for rnd 4, color G for rnd 5, color C for rnd 6.

FINISHING

Work 2 more rnds on each Paisley as foll: With RS facing, join K to ch at back of picot, ch 3, dc in same st, 2 dc in back of each picot of last rnd. Join by sl st into 3rd ch of rnd. Fasten off. Join MC to first st of rnd, ch 4, working in *back* loop of each st only, tr into each st of rnd, join with sl st to beg of rnd. Fasten off. Arrange Paisley A, B and C into triangle formation with pointed ends facing center as illustrated. With MC, RS facing and yarn held to back, work into front loop of edge st on one piece then front loop of edge st on other piece and slip st edges together. When the 12 pieces have been formed into 4 triangles, arrange them into a large triangle as illustrated: 3 right side up at each corner and 1 upside down in the center. Slip st them together.

MOTIF LAYOUT

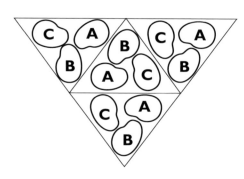

This skinny vintage-inspired crocheted scarf has an embossed entwining cable and mesh points with tassels at both ends. Designed by Ann E. Smith.

FINISHED MEASUREMENTS

FINISHED MEASUREMENTS

■ 3½"/9cm wide x 42"/106.5cm long, excluding tassels

MATERIALS

■ 2 1¾oz/50g hanks (each approx 210yd/193m) of Fiesta Yarns *La Luz* (silk) in #19 peach (**2**)
■ Size C/2 (2.5mm) crochet hook *or size to obtain gauge*

GAUGE

17 sts to 3"/7.5cm and 24 rows to 4"/10cm over sc pat st using size C/2 (2.5mm) hook.
Take time to check gauge.

STITCH GLOSSARY

Fpdc (front post dc) Work from front to back around post of dc or fpdc into 2nd row below to make a dc post st and skip the sc behind this fpdc.

SCARF
Ch 21.

Preparation rows
Row I (RS) Sc in 2nd ch from hook and each of next 3 ch, [dc in each of next 4 ch, sc in each of next 4 ch] twice—20 sts. Ch 1, turn.
Row 2 Sc in each sc and dc across. Ch 1, turn.
Row 3 Sc in first 3 sc, *fpdc over next 2 dc, skip 2 sc behind fpdc, sc in next 2 sc; rep from * across, ending last rep sc in last 3 sc. Ch 1, turn.
Row 4 Sc in each sc and fpdc across—20 sc. Ch 1, turn.
Row 5 Sc in first 3 sc, *fpdc over next 2 fpdc, skip 2 sc behind fpdc, sc in next 2 sc; rep from * across, ending last rep sc in last 3 sc. Ch 1, turn.
Row 6 Rep row 4.

CABLE PANEL

Row I Sc in first 2 sc, [fpdc over fpdc] twice, skip 2 sc behind fpdc, sc in each of next 4 sc, fpdc over next 4 fpdc and skip 4 sc behind fpdc, sc in next 4 sc, [fpdc over fpdc] twice and skip 2 sc behind fpdcs, sc in last 2 sc. Ch 1, turn.
Row 2 and all WS rows Sc in each sc and fpdc across—20 sc. Ch 1, turn.
Row 3 Sc in first 2 sc, fpdc over 2 fpdc and skip 2 sc behind fpdc, sc in 4 sc, skip next 2 fpdc, fpdc over third and fourth fpdc, fpdc over first then second skipped fpdc—cable made, skip 4 sc behind fpdc, sc in 4 sc, fpdc over 2 fpdc, skip 2 sc behind fpdc, sc in last 2 sc. Ch 1, turn.
Row 5 Rep row 1.

Row 7 Rep row 1.

Row 9 Rep row 3.

Row 11 Sc in first 3 sc, *fpdc over next 2 fpdc, skip 2 sc behind fpdc, sc in next 2 sc; rep from * across, ending last rep sc in last 3 sc. Ch 1, turn.

Row 13 Sc in first 4 sc, [fpdc over next 4 fpdc, skip 4 sc behind fpdc, sc in next 4 sc] twice. Ch 1, turn.

Row 15 Sc in first 4 sc, [cable over next 4 fpdc, and skip 4 sc behind fpdc, sc in next 4 sc] twice. Ch 1, turn.

Row 17 Rep row 13.

Row 19 Rep row 13.

Row 21 Rep row 15.

Row 23 Rep row 11.

Row 24 Rep row 2.

Rep cable panel rows 1-24 for 7 times in total, then rep rows 1-13 once, rep row 2 and row 13. Fasten off.

(make 2)

With the RS facing, work 19 sc evenly along edge. Do *not* turn. Working from left to right, *ch 2, skip next sc, sc in next sc; rep from * across—9 ch-2 lps. Ch 2, turn.

Row 2 Skip first ch-2 lp, *sc in next ch-2 lp, ch 2; rep from * across, ending sc in last ch-2 lp. Ch 2, turn.

Rep row 2 until 2 ch-2 lps rem. Ch 2, turn.

Last row Skip first ch-2 lp, sl st in next ch-2 lp and fasten off.

Make two 3½"/9cm tassels and attach one to each ch-2 lp at points of border.

Fine lightweight merino wool is paired with a fine gauge crochet hook to create a dense-bodied scarf in a slanting popcorn stitch pattern. Although it is precise and pretty in this scaled down size, the scarf could stretch to any length using additional balls of yarn. Designed by Mari Lynn Patrick.

FINISHED MEASUREMENTS
Approx 6"/15cm x 44"/112cm

MATERIALS
3 1¾oz/50g balls (each approx 189yd/175m) of Rowan Yarns *4-ply Soft* (wool) in #379 lt green (1)
Size E/4 (3.5mm) crochet hook *or size to obtain gauge*

GAUGE
6 popcorns and 13 rows to 4"/10cm over popcorn pattern stitch using size E/4 (3.5mm) hook.
Take time to check gauge.

POPCORN PATTERN STITCH
Chain a multiple of 3 ch plus 2 extra ch.

Row 1 (RS) Work 1 sc in 2nd ch from hook, 1 sc in each ch to end. Ch 1, turn.

Row 2 (WS) Work 1 sc in first sc, *work 1 popcorn by (yo hook, draw up a lp in sc) 5 times in next sc, yo and through all lps on hook, 1 sc in each of next 2 sc; rep from * to end. Ch 1, turn.

Row 3 Work 1 sc in each st to end. Ch 1, turn.

Row 4 *Work 1 sc in each of next 2 sc, work 1 popcorn in next sc; rep from *, end 1 sc in last sc. Ch 1, turn.

Row 5 Rep row 3.

Rep rows 2-5 for popcorn pattern stitch.

SCARF
Chain 29. Work popcorn pattern stitch on 9 popcorns until piece measures 44"/112cm from beg, end with pat row 2 or 4. Fasten off. Return to beg ch of scarf and working from WS, work pat row 4 into beg ch (this will give a matching popcorn edge at beg of scarf to look the same as end of scarf).

FINISHING
Block very lightly, if necessary, from WS.

Blue heaven

■■■■▶

This triangle neck scarf is worked in a year-round cotton yarn with open, lacy point joinings and a crown point edging. Designed by Gayle Bunn.

FINISHED MEASUREMENTS
■ Approx 41"/104cm wide along top of triangle and 21"/53cm deep

MATERIALS
■ 5 1¾oz/50g balls (each approx 136yd/125m) of Patons® *Grace* (cotton) in #60104 blue (**2**)
■ Size F/5 (3.75mm) crochet hook *or size to obtain gauge*

GAUGE
One motif is 3"/7.5cm square.
Take time to check gauge.

FIRST FULL MOTIF

Ch 5, join with a sl st to first ch to form ring.

Rnd 1 Ch 3 (counts as 1 dc), work 15 dc in ring, join with a sl st to top of ch-3—16 dc.

Rnd 2 Ch 3, (yo and draw up a loop, yo and draw through 2 loops on hook) twice in same sp as last sl st, yo and draw through all loops on hook (one cluster), *ch 3, (yo and draw up a loop, yo and draw through 2 loops on hook) 3 times in next dc, yo and draw through all loops on hook (for one cluster); rep from * around, ending with ch 3. Join with sl st to top of first cluster.

Rnd 3 Sl st in each of next 2 ch, ch 1, 1 sc in same sp, *ch 5, 1 sc in next ch-3 sp, (work 5 dc, ch 5, 5 dc) in next ch-3 sp, 1 sc in next ch-3 sp, ch 5**, 1 sc in next ch-3 sp, rep from * twice more, then rep from * to ** once. Sl st in first sc. Fasten off.

JOINING MOTIFS

All of the rem full motifs will be joined tog foll motif layout and working rnd 3 as foll: Sl st in each of next 2 ch, ch 1, 1 sc in same sp, *ch 2, sl st in corresponding ch-5 sp of adjoining motif, ch 2, 1 sc in next ch-3 sp, (work 5 dc, ch 2, sl st in corresponding ch-5 sp of adjoining motif, ch 2, 5 dc) in next ch-3 sp, 1 sc in next ch-3 sp, ch 2, sl st in corresponding ch-5 sp of adjoining motif, ch 2**, 1 sc in next ch-3 sp; rep from * twice more, then rep from * to ** once. Sl st in first sc. Fasten off.

HALF MOTIF

Ch 4, join with a sl st to first ch to form ring.
Note Half motif will be continued in rows, turning and working back and forth.

Row 1 Ch 3 (counts as 1 dc), work 7 dc in ring—8 dc. Turn.

Row 2 Ch 3, (yo and draw up a loop, yo and draw through 2 loops on hook) twice in same sp as last sl st, yo and draw through all loops on hook (one cluster), *ch 3, work cluster in next dc; rep from * across. Turn.

Row 3 Ch 3, sl st in corresponding corner of adjoining motif, 4 dc in first cluster, 1 sc in next ch-3 sp, [ch 2, sl st in corresponding ch-5 sp of adjoining motif, ch 2, 1 sc in next ch-3 sp] twice, (5 dc, ch 2, sl st in corresponding ch-5 sp of adjoining motif, ch 2, 5 dc) in next ch-3 sp, 1 sc in next ch-3 sp, [ch 2, sl st in corresponding ch-5 sp of adjoining motif, ch 2, 1 sc in next ch-3 sp] twice, 5 dc in last cluster, sl st in corresponding corner of adjoining motif. Fasten off. Work in this way until all motifs are joined foll motif layout.

FINISHING

Block lightly, if desired.

EDGING

Rnd 1 From RS, join yarn with a sl st to top right corner of half motif. Working along top edge, work ch 3 (counts as 1 dc), 24 dc across remainder of first half motif, work 25 dc across each of the rem 8 half motifs, 3 dc in corner, 16 dc down side of half motif, [1 dc in joining sp between motifs, 17 dc down side of next motif] 8 times, 5 dc in lower triangle point, [17 dc up side of next motif, 1 dc in joining sp between motifs] 8 times, 16 dc up side of half motif, 3 dc in corner. Join with sl st to top of ch-3. Fasten off.

Row 2 From RS, join yarn with a sl st to center dc at top of left corner. Ch 1, 1 sc in same sp with joining, *ch 5, [yo twice and draw up a loop, (yo and draw through 2 looks on hook) twice] 3 times in next dc, yo and through all loops on hook, (for tr cluster), ch 3, sl st in first ch (for picot), skip next 3 dc, 1 tr cluster in next dc, ch 5, 1 sc in each of next 2 dc; rep from * down left side and up right side of triangle, ending last rep with 1 sc in corner dc of right corner. Fasten off.

MOTIF LAYOUT

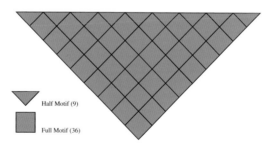

Half Motif (9)

Full Motif (36)

Circle in the square

■■■■▭

These **bulky squares** get some relief from their allover weight with single corner joinings. A trim and tiny scallop edge lend a light touch to this stole designed by Ann E. Smith.

FINISHED MEASUREMENTS
■ Approx 19"/48cm wide x 73"/185cm long, unstretched, 4 squares wide by 16 squares long

MATERIALS
■ 20 1¾oz/50g balls (each approx 64yd/58m) of Anny Blatt *Rustique* (wool) in #156 blue green (■)
■ Size G/6 (4.5mm) crochet hook *or size to obtain gauge*

GAUGE
One square is 4½"/11.5cm.

STITCH GLOSSARY
Puff stitch In next ch-1 sp (yo and draw up a lp) 3 times, yo and pull through all 7 lps on hook.

STEP 1 FIRST SQUARE

Ch 5, join with sl st to first ch to form ring.
Rnd 1 (RS) Ch 5 (counts as 1 tr and ch-1), [work 1 tr, ch 1] 11 times in ring—12 tr.

Join with a sl st in 4th ch of beg ch-5.
Rnd 2 (Work puff st, ch 1) twice in each ch-1 sp around—24 puff sts. Join with a sl st to first puff st.
Note On next rnd, each ch-1 sp and sp between 2 puff sts will be referred to as 1 sp.
Rnd 3 Sl st in next ch-1 sp, ch 6 (counts as 1 tr and ch-2), 1 tr in same sp (first corner made), *ch 1, 1 dc in next sp, [ch 1, 1 hdc in next sp] 3 times, ch 1, 1dc in next sp**, ch 1, (work 1 tr, ch 2, 1 tr) in next sp for corner; rep from * around, ending last rep at **, ch 1, join with a sl st in 4th ch of beg ch-6. Fasten off.

STEP 2 JOIN ONE SIDE SQUARE

Work as for first square through rnd 2.
Rnd 3 Sl st in next sp, ch 6 (counts as 1 tr and ch 2), 1 tr in same sp, *ch 1, 1 dc in next sp, [ch 1, 1 hdc in next sp] 3 times, ch 1, 1 dc in next sp**, ch 1, (1 tr, ch 2, 1 tr) in next sp for corner; rep from * to ** once, (for corner connection, work ch 1, 1 tr, ch 1 in next sp, holding square to left of last square made, drop ch-1 from hook, insert hook from back to front into corresponding corner sp, ch 1, 1 tr in same sp as last tr to complete corner), rep from * to **, make corner connecton; rep from * to **, ch 1, join and fasten off. Make 14 more squares as for step 2 (there are 16 squares in first strip).

Second strip

Make step 2 joining first square of strip 2 to first square of first strip.

Work as for first square through rnd 2.

STEP 3 JOIN TWO SIDES OF SQUARE

Rnd 3 Sl st in next ch-1 sp, ch 6 (counts as 1 tr and ch-2), 1 tr in same sp, *ch 1, 1 dc in next sp, [ch 1, 1 hdc in next sp] 3 times, ch 1, 1 dc in next sp**, work corner connection to last square made; rep from * to **; for 2nd connection, work ch 1, 1 tr, ch 1 in next sp, (drop ch-1 from hook, insert hook from back to front in corresponding corner sp, ch 1, drop ch-1 from hook, insert hook from back to front in corresponding sp of adjacent square, ch 1, 1 tr in same sp as last tr to

complete corner), rep from * to **; for 3rd connection, join to same square as last connection and in corresponding corner, rep from * to ** once more, join and fasten off. Make 14 more squares as for step 3.

Strips 3 and 4

Work through rnd 2 on first square, then work step 3 joining 2 sides of squares for 2 more strips of 16 squares each.

BORDER

With RS facing join with a sl st in any corner ch-2 sp, ch 3, sl st in same sp, *ch 3, sl st in next sp; rep from * around working (ch 3, 1 sl st, ch 3, 1 sl st) in each corner sp, end with ch 3, 1 sl st in first sl st. Fasten off.

MOTIF LAYOUT

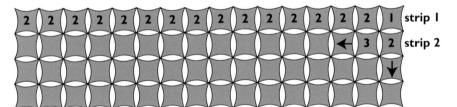

Whimsical novelty tape yarn is paired with dyed-to-match eyelash yarn to create an allover confetti and feather look for this distinctive neck scarf. Designed by Karen Klemp.

FINISHED MEASUREMENTS

Approx 44"/112cm wide along top of triangle and 21"/53cm deep after stretching and blocking

MATERIALS

3 .70oz/20g balls (each approx 70yd/64m) of Trendsetter Yarns *Flora* (viscose/polyester) in #22 pink multi (A) **5**

3 .70oz/20g balls (each approx 77yd/70m) of Trendsetter Yarns *Shadow* (polyester) in #1007 pink multi (B) **5**

Size N (10mm) crochet hook *or size to obtain gauge*

GAUGE

6 dc and 6 rows to 4" over dc pat using A and B held tog and size N (10mm) crochet hook worked very loosely.
Take time to check gauge.

Note The extra large hook size used to work this simple dc pat st scarf gives an openwork fishnet appearance. It is not recommended to change hook sizes to obtain the stated gauge. Only work the gauge swatch with a looser or tighter tension to achieve the look of the fabric for this style.

SCARF

Beg at lower point of triangle, with 1 strand A and B held tog, ch 3.

Row 1 Work 2 dc in 3rd ch from hook, turn.

Row 2 Ch 2 (counts as 1 dc), 1 dc in first st, 1 dc in next st, 2 dc in top of t-ch, turn.

Row 3 Ch 2, 1 dc in first st, 1 dc in each dc across, end 2 dc in top of t-ch of previous row, turn.

Rep row 3 for dc pat until all yarn has been used. There should be 59 dc. Fasten off.

FINISHING

Block to finished measurements, stretching to achieve the fishnet openwork effect.

■■■▢

Shades of blue and green—in two colors of a marled brushed mohair yarn— amplify this nubby textured scarf. Designed by Katherine Fedewa.

FINISHED MEASUREMENTS
▢ Approx 6½"/16.5cm wide x 64"/ 162.5cm long, excluding fringe

MATERIALS
▢ 2 2½ oz/70g balls (each approx 222yd/ 203m) of Lion Brand Yarn Company *Imagine* (acrylic/mohair) each in #171 moss (A) and #328 blue (B) (▣4)
▢ Size I/9 (5.5mm) crochet hook *or size to obtain gauge*

GAUGE
12 sts to 4"/10cm and 11 rows to 6"/15cm over pat st using 1 strand of A and B held tog and size I/9 (5.5mm) crochet hook. *Take time to check gauge.*

STITCH GLOSSARY
Hdc2tog *Yo, insert hook into st, yo and pull up a lp (3 lps on hook); rep from * once more in same st, yo and through all 5 lps on hook, yo and draw lp through to finish.
Dc2tog Work 1 dc in next ch-1 sp until 2 lps rem on hook, work a 2nd dc into next ch-1 sp until 3 lps rem on hook, yo and through all 3 lps on hook.

PATTERN STITCH
Ch a multiple of 6 ch plus 2 extra
Row 1 Work 1 sc in 2nd ch from hook, *ch 1, skip 2 ch, in next ch work (hdc2tog, ch 1) 3 times, skip 2 ch, 1 sc in next ch; rep from * to end, turn.

Row 2 Ch 4 (counts as 1 dc and ch 1), skip first ch-1 sp, 1 sc in next ch-1 sp, ch 3, 1 sc in next ch-1 sp, *ch 1, dc2tog over next 2 ch-1 sps, ch 1, 1 sc in next ch-1 sp, ch 3, 1 sc in next ch-1 sp; rep from * to last sc, skip last ch-1 sp, ch 1, 1 dc in last sc, turn.

Row 3 Ch 3 (counts as 1 hdc and ch 1), hdc2tog in first dc, ch 1, 1 sc in next ch-3 sp, ch 1, *in top of next dc2tog work (hdc2tog, ch 1) 3 times, 1 sc in next ch-3 sp, ch 1; rep from * to t-ch, in 3rd ch of ch-4 at beg of previous row work (hdc2tog, 1 hdc), turn.

Row 4 Ch 1, 1 sc in first hdc, 1 sc in first ch-1 sp, ch 1, dc2tog over next 2 ch-1 sp, ch 1, *1 sc in next ch-1 sp, ch 3, 1 sc in next ch-1 sp, ch 1, dc2tog over next 2 ch-1 sps, ch 1; rep from *, end 1 sc in 2nd ch of t-ch, turn.

Row 5 Ch 1, 1 sc in first sc, *ch 1, in top of next dc2tog work (hdc2tog, ch 1) 3 times, 1 sc in next ch-3 sp; rep from * end placing last sc in last sc, turn.

Rep rows 2-5 for pattern st.

SCARF
With 1 strand each A and B held tog, ch 20. Work in pat st until scarf measures 64"/62.5cm from beg.

FINISHING
Lightly block scarf.

FRINGE
Cut 11"/28cm length of yarn for each fringe. Alternate 3 strands of A for 1 fringe, 3 strands of B for 2nd fringe and 2 strands of A and 1 of B for third fringe and place 11 fringe along each end of scarf.

PATCHWORK SHAWL
Blast from the past

A set of non-repeating color squares in two different pattern combinations lend timeless appeal to this granny square shawl. Designed by **Mari Lynn Patrick**, it also features black openwork mesh joinings.

FINISHED MEASUREMENTS

Approx 79"/200cm wide along top of triangle and 43"/109cm deep

MATERIALS

8 1¾oz/50g hanks (each approx 88yd/80m) of Brown Sheep Yarn Company *Handpaint Originals* (wool/mohair) in #HP25 black (A) ▰

4 hanks in #HP85 cream (B)

3 hanks in #40 red multi (C)

2 hanks each #HP05 plum (D) and #HP35 chestnut (E)

1 hank each in #HP45 lt purple (F) and #HP95 cranberry (G)

Size G/7 (4.5mm) crochet hook *or size to obtain gauge*

GAUGE

Square A is 5½"/14cm square, including black edge.

Take time to check gauge.

SQUARE A

Make a total of 22 in colors as described later. Ch 4, join with sl st to form ring.

Rnd 1 [Work 1 sc in ring, ch 3] 4 times, join with sl st to first sc.

Rnd 2 Sl st in ch-3 sp, ch 3 (counts as 1 dc), 2 dc, ch 3 and 3 dc in same sp for corner, *3 dc, ch 3 and 3 dc in next sp; rep from * twice, join with sl st to top of ch-3. Fasten off.

Rnd 3 With loop on hook, 1 sc in a corner ch-2 sp, ch 3, 1 sc in same sp, *ch 3, 1 sc between next 3rd and 4th dc's, ch 3, 1 sc, ch 3 and 1 sc in corner; rep from *, end ch 3, join with sl st to first sc.

Rnd 4 Sl st in corner ch-3 sp, ch 3 (counts as 1 dc), 2 dc, ch 3 and 3 dc in corner, *3 dc in each ch-3 sp to next corner, 3 dc, ch 3 and 3 dc in corner; rep from *, end 3 dc in last sp, join to top of first ch-3. Fasten off.

Rnd 5 With loop on hook, 1 sc in corner sp, ch 3, 1 sc in same sp, *ch 3, 1 sc between each of the next 3rd and 4th dc's to next corner, 1 sc, ch 3 and 1 sc in corner; rep from *, end ch 3, join with sl st to first sc.

Rnd 6 Rep rnd 4.

Rnd 7 With black (A) on all squares, *work sc in one sp between 3 dc group, ch 5; rep from * to corner, work sc, ch 7 and sc in corner, ch 5; rep from * around. Join to first sc. Fasten off.

SQUARE B

Make a total of 6 in colors as described later. Ch 6, join with sl st to form ring.

Rnd 1 Ch 3 (counts as 1 dc), work 15 dc in ring, join with sl st first dc. Fasten off.

Rnd 2 With loop on hook, work 1 dc in any dc, ch 2, *1 dc in next dc, ch 2; rep from * around—16 dc and ch-2 sps. Join with sl st to top of first dc. Fasten off.

Rnd 3 With loop on hook, work 2 dc in any ch-2 sp for start of corner, *ch 1, [2 dc in next sp, ch 1] 4 times, ch 3 for corner, 2 dc in same corner sp; rep from * ending ch 1, [2 dc in next sp, ch 1] 4 times, ch 3 for corner, join with sl st to top of dc. Fasten off.

Rnd 4 With loop on hook, 1 sc in corner ch-3 sp, ch 3, 1 sc in same sp, *ch 3, 1 sc in 2nd dc of 2 dc group; rep from * twice, ch 3, 1 sc, ch 3 and 1 sc in corner; rep from * around, end ch 3, join with sl st to top of first sc. Fasten off.

Rnd 5 Work rnd 4 of square A.

Rnd 6 Work rnd 7 of square A.

TRIANGLE C

Make a total of 8 in colors as described later. Ch 4, join with sl st to form ring.

Row 1 [Work 1 sc in ring, ch 3] 3 times, 1 sc in ring, turn.

Row 2 Ch 3 (counts as 1 dc), 3 dc in ch 3-sp, 3 dc, ch 3 and 3 dc in corner sp, 3 dc in last sp, Fasten off. Turn.

Row 3 With loop on hook, sc in top of first dc, ch 3, sc in same st, [ch 3, sc between next 3rd and 4th dc's] twice, ch 3, sc in same corner sp, [ch 3, sc between next 3rd and 4th dc's] twice, ch 3, sc in same sp as last sc, turn.

Row 4 Ch 3 (counts as 1 dc), 2 dc in first ch-3 sp, 3 dc in each ch-3 sp to corner, 3 dc, ch 3 and 3 dc in corner, 3 dc in each ch-3 sp to end. Fasten off. Turn.

Row 5 With loop on hook, sc in top of first dc, ch 3, sc in same st, *ch 3, sc between next 3rd and 4th dc's to corner, ch 3, sc, ch 3, sc in corner sp; rep from *, end ch 3, sc in same dc as last sc. Turn.

Row 6 Rep row 4.

Row 7 With black (A), work sc in first dc, ch 7, sc in same dc, *ch 5, sc between 3rd and 4th dc's; rep from * to corner, ch 7, sc in corner, rep from * to end. Fasten off.

COLOR SEQUENCE

Note All final rnds are worked with black (A) foll instructions for squares.

Square A1

Beg with plum (D), work rnds 1 and 2 with D, rnd 3 with cream (B), rnd 4 with plum (D), rnd 5 with cream (B), rnd 6 with lt purple (F).

Square B2

Beg with black (A), work rnd 1 with A, rnd 2 with cream (B), rnd 3 with cranberry (G), rnd 4 with cream (B), rnd 5 with chestnut (E).

Square A3

Beg with chestnut (E), work rnds 1 and 2 with E, rnds 3 and 4 with cream (B), rnds 5 and 6 with plum (D).

Square A4

Beg with cranberry (G), work rnds 1-4 with G, rnd 5 with lt purple (F), rnd 6 with cranberry (G).

Square A5
Beg with lt purple (F), work rnds 1 and 2 with F, rnds 3 and 4 with plum (D), rnds 5 and 6 with lt purple (F).

Square A6
Beg with plum (D), work rnd 1 with D, rnd 2 with chestnut (E), rnd 3 with D, rnd 4 with E, rnd 5 with D, rnd 6 with E.

Square A7
Beg with cranberry (G), work rnds 1-4 with G, rnd 5 with cream (B), rnd 6 with lt purple (F).

Square B8
Beg with plum (D), work rnd 1 with D, rnd 2 with lt purple (F), rnd 3 with cream (B), rnd 4 with plum (D), rnd 5 with cream (B).

Square B9
Beg with cream (B), work rnd 1 with B, rnd 2 with black (A), rnd 3 with red multi (C), rnd 4 with chestnut (E), rnd 5 with cranberry (G).

Square A10
Beg with black (A), work rnds 1 and 2 with A, rnd 3 with chestnut (E), rnd 4 with cranberry (G), rnd 5 with cream (B), rnd 6 with red multi (C).

Square B11
Beg with red multi (C), work rnd 1 with C, rnd 2 with chestnut (E), rnd 3 with C, rnds 4 and 5 with E.

Square A12
Beg with chestnut (E), work rnds 1 and 2 with E, rnd 3 with cream (B), rnd 4 with E, rnd 5 with B, rnd 6 with plum (D).

Square A13
Beg with cream (B), work rnds 1 and 2 with B, rnds 3 and 4 with cranberry (G), rnds 5 and 6 with red multi (C).

Square A14
Beg with black (A), work rnd 1 with A, rnds 2-4 with red multi (C), rnd 5 with A, rnd 6 with plum (D).

Square A15
Beg with black (A), work rnd 1 with A, rnd 2 with plum (D), rnds 3 and 4 with cream (B), rnd 5 with cranberry (G), rnd 6 with B.

Square B16
Beg with cranberry (G), work rnd 1 with G, rnd 2 with cream (B), rnd 3 with lt purple (F), rnds 4 and 5 with red multi (C).

Square A17
Beg with cream (B), work rnd 1 with B, rnd 2 with chestnut (E), rnds 3 and 4 with plum (D), rnd 5 with black (A), rnd 6 with cream (B).

Square A18
Beg with red multi (C), work rnd 1 with C, rnd 2 with lt purple (F), rnds 3 and 4 with cranberry (G), rnd 5 with chestnut (E), rnd 6 with G.

Square A19

Beg with red multi (C), work rnd 1 with C, rnd 2 with cream (B), rnds 3 and 4 with C, rnd 5 with B, rnd 6 with C.

Square A20

Beg with chestnut (E), work rnd 1 with E, rnd 2 with lt purple (F), rnds 3 and 4 with plum (D), rnd 5 with chestnut (E), rnd 6 with lt purple (F).

Square B21

Beg with cream (B), work rnd 1 with B, rnd 2 with chestnut (E), rnd 3 with plum (D), rnds 4 and 5 with cranberry (G).

Square A22

Beg with chestnut (E), work rnd 1 with E, rnd 2 with black (A), rnd 3 with E, rnd 4 with cranberry (G), rnd 5 with lt purple (F), rnd 6 with plum (D).

Square A23

Beg with black (A), work rnds 1 and 2 with A, rnd 3 with lt purple (F), rnd 4 with plum (D), rnd 5 with cream (B), rnd 6 with red multi (C).

Square A24

Beg with red multi (C), work rnd 1 with C, rnd 2 with plum (D), rnd 3 with C, rnd 4 with D, rnd 5 with C, rnd 6 with D.

Square A25

Beg with plum (D), work rnds 1 and 2 with D, rnds 3 and 4 with red multi (C), rnd 5 with lt purple (F), rnd 6 with chestnut (E).

Square A26

Beg with cream (B), work rnd 1 with B, rnd 2 with red multi (C), rnds 3 and 4 with B, rnd 5 with black (A), rnd 6 with plum (D).

Square A27

Beg with red multi (C), work rnds 1 and 2 with C, rnds 3 and 4 with black (A), rnds 5 and 6 with C.

Square A28

Beg with chestnut (E), work rnds 1 and 2 with E, rnds 3 and 4 with cranberry (G), rnd 5 with black (A), rnd 6 with cream (B).

Triangle C1

Beg with cream (B), work rows 1 and 2 with B, rows 3 and 4 with red multi (C), row 5 with B, row 6 with cranberry (G).

Triangle C2

Beg with black (A), work row 1 with A, row 2 with red multi (C), row 3 with A, row 4 with chestnut (E), row 5 with lt purple (F), row 6 with E.

Triangle C3

Beg with cranberry (G), work rows 1 and 2 with G, row 3 with lt purple (F), row 4 with chestnut (E), row 5 with F, row 6 with G.

Triangle C4

Beg with black (A), work rows 1 and 2 with A, row 3 with red multi (C), row 4 with chestnut (E), row 5 with C, row 6 with plum (D).

Triangle C5

Beg with plum (D), work rows 1 and 2 with D, row 3 with cream (B), row 4 with chestnut (E), row 5 with B, row 6 with cranberry (G).

Triangle C6

Beg with red multi (C), work rows 1 and 2 with C, row 3 with black (A), row 4 with cream (B), row 5 with A, row 6 with C.

Triangle C7

Beg with lt purple (F), work rows 1 and 2 with F, row 3 with plum (D), row 4 with F, row 5 with D, row 6 with F.

Triangle C8

Beg with chestnut (E), work rows 1 and 2 with E, row 3 with plum (D), row 4 with E, rows 5 and 6 with red multi (C).

FINISHING

Lay out motifs foll diagram.

JOIN SQUARES

To join squares, using black (A), *sc in corner lp of one square, ch 2, sc in corresponding lp of adjoining square; rep from * until sides of square are joined. To join squares at center point of 4 squares, work a ch-2 joining to 2 diagonally opposite squares, then a ch-3 joining with 2nd ch worked through the center of this joining.

EDGING

Rnd 1 Join black (A) in top right corner of C1 triangle, *ch 5, sc in top of C1 triangle; rep from * 9 times more across top of C1 triangle, rep from * across all triangles at top of shawl, work ch 5, sc in top corner lp, then work ch 5, sc in each ch-5 lp down side of triangle, sc, ch 5, sc in triangle point, then ch 5, sc in each ch-5 lp up side of triangle, sc, ch 5, join with sc to first sc.

Rnd 2 Ch 5, sc in ch-5 corner lp, *ch 3, sc in each ch-5 lp to corner, ch 3, sc in ch-5 corner sp, ch 5, sc in corner; rep from * around.

Rnd 3 Ch 7, sc in corner ch-5 lp, *ch 5, sc in each ch-3 lp to corner, ch 5, sc in ch-5 corner sp, ch 7, sc in corner; rep from * around.

Rnd 4 Rep rnd 2.

Rnd 5 With cream (B), work 3 dc in each ch-5 lp and (3 dc, ch 2, 3 dc) in each corner sp.

Rnd 6 Rep rnd 2.

Rnd 7 With red multi (C), rep rnd 5.

Rnd 8 Rep rnd 2.

Rnd 9 Rep rnd 5.

Rnd 10 Rep rnd 2.

Fasten off.

MOTIF LAYOUT

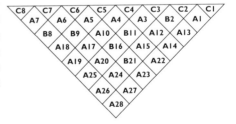

A **close-ribbed neck edge serves to hold the scarf in place snugly around the neck. Easy to crochet, this heirloom scarf makes a stunning statement from day to night. Designed by Candace Eisner Strick.**

FINISHED MEASUREMENTS
Approx 6½"/16.5cm wide at lower edges and 48"/122cm long

MATERIALS
3 .88oz/25g skeins (each approx 150yd/135m) of Jamiesons *2-Ply Spindrift* (wool) in #153 pink heather (⓵)
Size E/4 (3.5mm) crochet hook *or size to obtain gauge*

GAUGE
12 sts and 16 rows to 2"/5cm over neck ribbing pat using size E/4 (3.5mm) hook. *Take time to check gauge.*

Note The neck ribbing is worked lengthwise then each lace strip is worked downwards from the side (or row) edges of the neck ribbing.

SCARF
Neck ribbing
Ch 80.

Row 1 Work 2 sc in 3rd ch from hook, work 1 sc in each rem ch to end. Ch 1, turn.

Row 2 Skip the first sc, insert hook into the *back* loop only of next st and work 1 sc through back lp (tbl), work 1 sc tbl in each sc to end, work 1 sc tbl in the t-ch. Ch 1, turn. Rep row 2 until there are 29 rows. Do *not* turn work after last rib row.

FIRST LACE STRIP
Set-up row
Working along side of ribbed piece (into sides of rows), ch 3, 1 dc in next ridge, 1 dc in next ridge, *skip 1 furrow, ([work 1 dc, ch 1] 3 times, 1 dc) in next furrow*; rep between *'s to last 2 furrows, skip 1 furrow, 2 dc in last ridge—6 clusters made, turn.

Next row Ch 3, 1 dc in 2nd dc, *([work 1 dc, ch 1] 3 times, 1 dc) in middle of ch-1 sp of cluster; rep from *, end 2 dc in last sp. Rep this row until lace strip measures 15"/38cm. Join yarn to opposite edge of neck ribbing and work 2nd lace strip in same way.

FINISHING
Wash scarf in cool water. Do not wring or twist. Lay flat to block.

■■■■▭

Cluster rows worked in delicate mohair are separated by chain rows in a rayon tape to create this wave pattern stitch stole. Designed by Mari Lynn Patrick.

FINISHED MEASUREMENTS
■ Approx 18"/46cm wide x 78"/198cm long

MATERIALS
■ 6 1¾oz/50g balls (each approx 93yd/85m) of Berroco, Inc. *Mohair Classic* (mohair/wool/nylon) in #B1138 denim blue (A) 🔵

■ 5 1¾oz/50g hanks (each approx 75yd/69m) of Berroco, Inc. *Glacé* (rayon) in #2543 lt blue (B) 🔵

■ Size J/10 (6mm) crochet hook *or size to obtain gauge*

GAUGE
1 cluster pat and 6 pat rows to 3"/7.5cm. *Take time to check gauge.*

WAVE PATTERN STITCH
Ch a multiple of 12 sts plus 6 extra

Row 1 (RS) Work [1tr, ch 1] 3 times into 6th ch from hook, skip 5 ch, 1 sc in next ch, *ch 1, skip 5 ch, work [1 tr, ch 1] 7 times in next ch (for cluster), skip 5 ch, 1 sc in next ch; rep from * to last 6 ch, ch 1, work [1 tr, ch 1] 3 times in last ch, 1 tr in same ch as last 3 tr. Ch 1, turn.

Row 2 Work 1 sc in first tr, *ch 6, 1 sc in next sc, ch 6, skip 3 tr, 1 sc in next tr; rep from *, placing last sc into 4th ch of the ch 5 at beg of previous row. Ch 1, turn.

Row 3 Work 1 sc in first sc, *ch 6, 1 sc in next sc; rep from * to end. Ch 1, turn.

Row 4 Work 1 sc in first sc, *ch 1, work [1 tr, ch 1] 7 times in next sc, 1 sc in next sc; rep from * to end. Ch 1, turn.

Row 5 Work 1 sc in first sc, *ch 6, skip 3 tr, 1 sc in next tr, ch 6, 1 sc in next sc; rep from * to end. Ch 1, turn.

Row 6 Work 1 sc in first sc, *ch 6, 1 sc in next sc; rep from * to end. Ch 5, turn.

Row 7 Counting the ch 5 as 1 tr and ch 1, work [1 tr, ch 1] 3 times in first sc, 1 sc in next sc, *ch 1, work [1 tr, ch 1] 7 times in next sc, 1 sc in next sc; rep from * to last sc, work [ch 1, 1 tr] 4 times in last sc. Ch 1, turn.

Rep rows 2-7 for wave pattern st.

Notes

1 When changing colors from A to B, draw the new color through last 2 loops on hook and ch and turn at end of row with the new color.

2 In order to avoid cutting and rejoining of yarns when it is necessary at color changes, fasten off the old color and leave at end of row, then return to the opposite end to pick up the new color and work row from this new starting position.

STOLE
With size J/10 (6mm) hook and A, ch 78.
Rows 1-4 Work pat rows 1-4 with A.
Rows 5 and 6 Work pat rows 5 and 6 with B.

***Row 7** Work pat row 7 with A.

Rows 8 and 9 Work pat rows 2 and 3 with B.

Row 10 Work pat row 4 with A.

Rows 11 and 12 Work pat rows 5 and 6 with B.*

Rep between *'s (6-row pat rep) for color pat until piece measures approx 75"/ 190cm from beg, end with row 3 of wave pat st. Then with A only, work rows 4-7. Then with B, work row 2.

Last row Skip first sc, *work 1 sc in each of first 3 ch of ch-6 loop, ch 3, sl st in 3rd ch from hook (for picot), work 1 sc in each of next 3 ch of ch-6 loop, skip next sc; rep from * to end. Fasten off. Return to beg ch of stole and from RS, join B and work row 2 in beg ch sts across. With B, work last row as other end of stole. Fasten off.

FINISHING

Block stole from WS to measurements.

64

SPOKE MOTIF SHAWL
Olé!

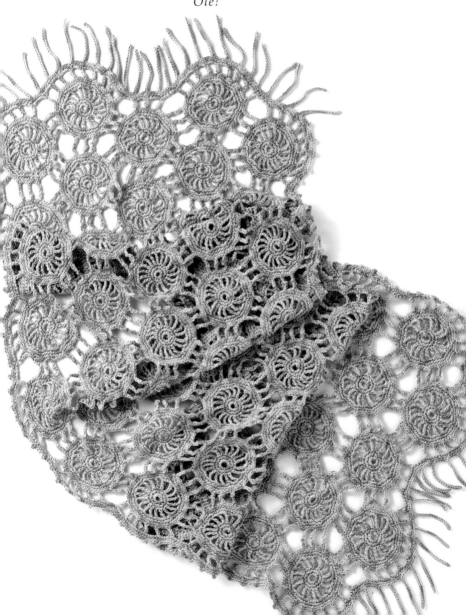

Circular spoke motifs are combined with triple chain joinings to create the allover airiness to this summer weight cotton shawl. Designed by Svetlana Avrakh in sunset shades of a cotton yarn.

FINISHED MEASUREMENTS
░ Approx 20"/51cm wide x 68"/173cm long, excluding chain fringe

MATERIALS
░ 9 1¾ oz/50g balls (each approx 136yd/ 125m) of Patons® *Grace* (cotton) in #60901 orange navigated (**2**)
░ Size E/4 (3.5mm) crochet hook or size *to obtain gauge*

GAUGE
One spiral motif is 4½"/11.5cm across. *Take time to check gauge.*

FIRST MOTIF
**Ch 6, join with sl st to first ch to form ring.
Rnd 1 Ch 1, 9 sc in ring. Join with sl st to first sc.
Rnd 2 Ch 1, 2 sc in each sc around. Join with sl st to first sc—18 sc.
Rnd 3 Ch 6 (counts as 1 tr and ch 2), skip first sc, [1 tr in next sc, ch 2] 17 times. Join with sl st to 4th ch of ch-6.
Rnd 4 Sl st in first ch-2 sp, ch 1, 2 sc in same sp as last sl st, *3 sc in next ch-2 sp, 2 sc in next ch-2 sp; rep from * to last ch-2 sp, 3 sc in last ch-2 sp. Join with sl st to first sc—45 sc.
Rnd 5 Ch 1, 1 sc in each of first 4 sc, *2 sc in next sc, 1 sc in each of next 4 sc; rep from * to last sc, 2 sc in last sc. Join with sl st to first sc—54 sc**.
Rnd 6 (picot round) Ch 1, 1 sc in each of first 3 sc, *ch 4, sl st in 2nd and 3rd ch from hook, sl st in top of last sc (picot), 1 sc in each of next 3 sc; rep from * around, work picot over last sc. Join with sl st to first sc. Fasten off.

SECOND MOTIF
Rep from ** to ** on first motif.
Rnd 6 Ch 1, 1 sc in each of first 3 sc, ch 3, sl st in top of picot of adjoining motif, sl st in 2nd and 3rd ch from hook, sl st in top of last sc (for joining picot), [1 sc in each of next 3 sc, joining picot in next picot of adjoining motif] twice, *1 sc in each of next 3 sc, work ch-4 picot; rep from * to end of rnd, end ch-4 picot over last sc. Join with sl st to first sc. Fasten off. Make 65 motifs as for 2nd motif and join as for motif layout.

EDGING
Rnd 1 Beg at top right motif, join yarn with a sl st to first loose picot, [ch 4, sl st in top of next picot] 8 times, *ch 5, [sl st in top of next picot, ch 4] twice, sl st in next picot, [ch 5, sl st in next picot, (ch 4, sl st in top of next picot) 8 times]* twice, **ch 5, sl st in next picot, [ch 4, sl st in next picot] 5 times**; rep from ** to ** 10 times more, [ch 5, (sl st in next picot, ch 4) 8 times] twice, sl st in next picot; rep from * to * once, rep from ** to ** 11

times more, ch 5, [sl st in top of next picot, ch 4] 8 times, sl st in top of next picot, ch 5, join with sl st to first sc.

Rnd 2 Ch 1, [4 sc in next ch-4 sp] 8 times, *5 sc in next ch-5 sp, [4 sc in next ch-4 sp] twice, [5 sc in next ch-5 sp. (4 sc in next ch-4 sp) 8 times]* twice, **5 sc in next ch-5 sp, [4 sc in next ch-4 sp] 5 times**; rep from ** to ** 10 times more, 5 sc in next ch-5 sp, (4 sc in next ch-4 sp] 8 times; rep from * to * once, rep from ** to ** 11 times more, 5 sc in next ch-5 sp, [4 sc in next ch-4 sp] 8 times, 5 sc in next ch-5 sp, join with sl st to first sc.

Rnd 3 (fringe edging) Ch 1, 1 sc in same sp as last sl st, 1 sc in next sc, [ch 17, 1 sl st in 2nd ch from hook and in each ch to end of ch, sl st in top of last sc for 1 fringe, 1 sc in each of next 4 sc] 24 times, *[ch 3, sl st in top of last sc for small picot, 1 sc in each of next 4 sc] 81 times*, [work 1 fringe, 1 sc in each of next 4 sc] 28 times, rep from * to * once more, [work 1 fringe, 1 sc in each of next 4 sc] 3 times, work 1 fringe, 1 sc in each sc to end of rnd. Join with sl st to first sc. Fasten off.

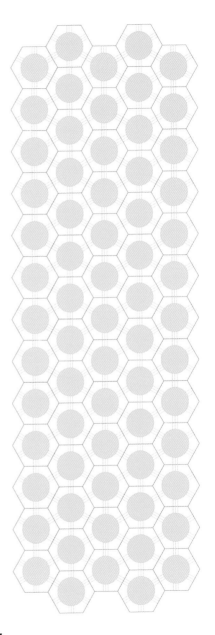

Two rows of a scallop pattern fit together to form a daisy chain motif that is worked in two striking alternating colors. Designed by Katherine Fedewa in a bulky weight yarn.

FINISHED MEASUREMENTS
Approx 5"/12.5cm wide x 67"/170cm long

MATERIALS
 4 1¾oz/50g balls (each approx 49yd/45m) of Zitron/Skacel Collection *Wellness* (wool/acrylic) in #48 dk red (A) (⬛)
 3 balls in #52 coral (B)
 Size K/10½ (7mm) crochet hook *or size to obtain gauge*

GAUGE
One 7-dc scallop to 2"/5cm and 4 rows scallop st to 3"/7.5cm over scallop pat st using size K/10½ (7mm) hook.
Take time to check gauge.

STITCH GLOSSARY
CL (cluster) Work (yo, insert hook into st, yo, draw loop through st, yo, draw through 2 loops) over the number of sts indicated, yo, draw through all loops on hook.

SCALLOP STITCH PATTERN
Ch a multiple of 10 plus 6 ch plus 1 extra for base ch.

Row 1 Work 1 sc in 2nd ch from hook, 1 sc in next ch, *skip 3 ch, 7 dc in next ch, skip 3 ch, 1 sc in each of next 3 ch; rep from * to last 4 ch, skip 3 ch, 4 dc in last ch. Ch 1, turn.

Row 2 Work 1 sc in each of first 2 sts, *ch 3, 1 CL over next 7 sts, ch 3, 1 sc in each of next 3 sts; rep from * to last 4 sts, ch 3, 1 CL over last 4 sts, skip t-ch. Ch 3, turn.

Row 3 Counting ch 3 as 1 dc, work 3 dc into first st, *skip ch-3 sp, 1 sc in each of next 3 sc, skip ch-3 sp, 7 dc into the loop that closed next CL; rep from *, end with skip ch-3 sp, 1 sc in each of last 2 sc, skip t-ch. Ch 3, turn.

Row 4 Counting ch 3 as 1 dc, skip first st, 1 CL over next 3 sts, *ch 3, 1 sc in each of next 3 sts, ch 3, 1 CL over next 7 sts; rep from *, end with ch 3, 1 sc in next st, 1 sc in top of t-ch. Ch 1, turn.

Row 5 Work 1 sc in each of first 2 sc, *skip ch-3 sp, 7 dc into the loop that closed next CL, skip ch-3 sp, 1 sc in each of next 3 sc; rep from *, end skip ch-3 sp, 4 dc in top of t-ch. Ch 1, turn.

Rep rows 2-5 for scallop stitch pattern.

SCARF
With A, ch 217. Work row 1 of scallop st pat. Change to B and work rows 2 and 3 of scallop st pat. Change to A and work rows 4 and 5 of scallop st pat. Fasten off.
Return to opposite side of scarf (base ch edge) and join A, beg at the end with 2 sc. With A, work row 5 of scallop st pat, working 7 dc into same ch-sp as 7 dc scallop of row 1. Change to B and work rows 2 and 3 of scallop st pat. Fasten off.

The natural affinity that crochet stitches lend to linear graphic design is expressed in this plaid double crochet stitch scarf. This type of plaid–known as buffalo check or buffalo plaid–is worked out in a design by Ann E. Smith.

Notes

1 When changing colors foll chart, work dc with chart designated color until only 2 loops rem on hook, draw the next color through these 2 loops on hook.
2 Work over color not in use so that color is carried along at top of last dc row while working.
3 When working chart rows 5-8, after completing last dc, ch 2 with same color first worked, then ch 1 with new color.

SCARF

With A, ch 37.
Row 1 (RS) Work 1 dc in 4th ch from hook, 1 dc in each of next 4 ch, 1 dc in next ch *drawing B through last 2 lps on hook, [work 1 dc with B drawing A through last 2 lps on hook, work 1 dc with A drawing B through last 2 lps on hook] 3 times, work 1 dc with B drawing A through last 2 loops on hook, work 1 dc in each of next 7 ch with A; rep from * once more. Ch 3, turn. This is the first row of the chart with the chain-3 at beg of row counting as 1 dc. Beg with row 2 of chart, cont to foll chart as set up, rep rows 1-8 a total of 14 times. Then, rep rows 1-4 once. Fasten off.

FINISHING

Block lightly, if necessary.

FRINGE

Cut each fringe 6"/15cm long (36 lengths of A and 32 lengths of B) using 2 lengths for each individual fringe and working 3 A fringe along each block in A and 4 B fringe to match each B stripe in 2-color block, attach fringe to each end of scarf as in photo.

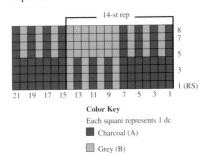

Color Key
Each square represents 1 dc
■ Charcoal (A)
■ Grey (B)

RIPPLE PATTERN SCARF

Sea breeze

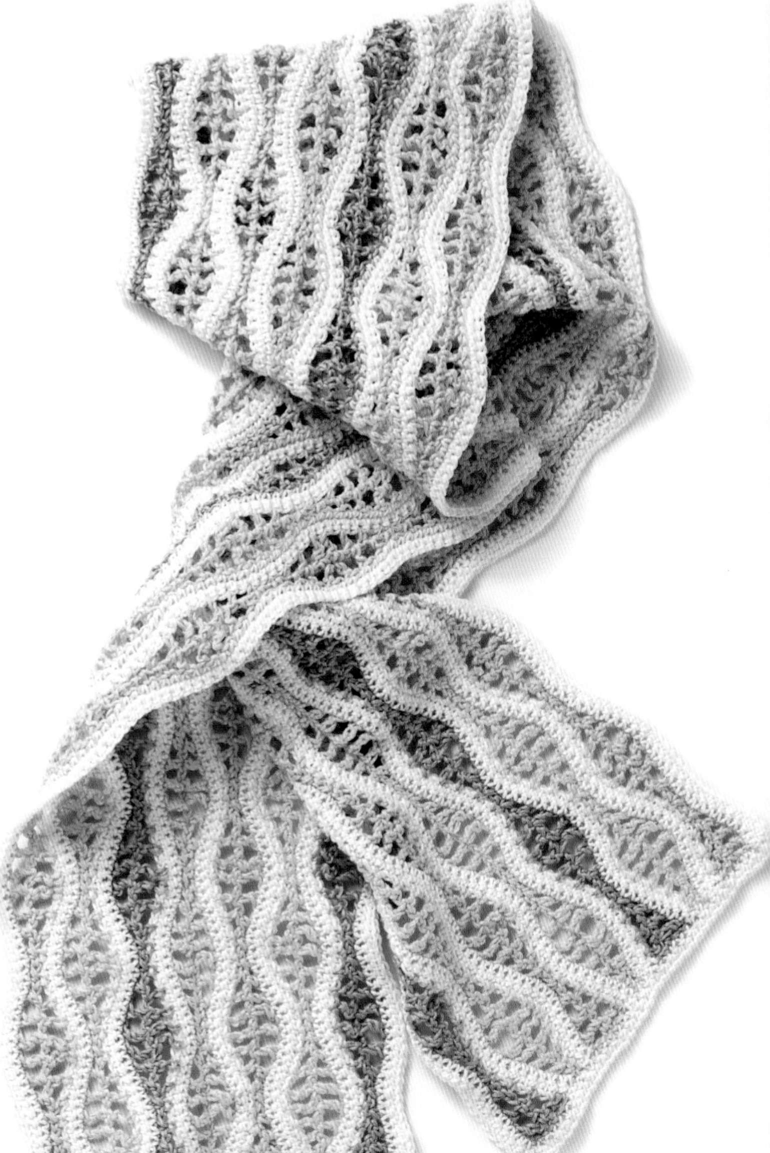

■■■▭

Designed by Ruthie Marks, this summer stunner showcases an allover ripple pattern stitched in creamy pastel hues. A white trim adds striking contrast.

FINISHED MEASUREMENTS
▨ Approx 7½"/19cm wide x 60"/152cm long

MATERIALS
▨ 20 1¾oz/50g balls (each approx 54yd/50m) of Sesia/LBUSA *Cable 2005* (cotton) in #51 white (A) 🔳
▨ 1 ball each in #99 yellow (B), #148 green (C) and #425 blue (D)
▨ Size C/2 (2.75mm) crochet hook *or size to obtain gauge*

GAUGE
20 sc and 16 rows to 4"/10cm over sc pat st using size C/2 (2.75mm) hook.
Take time to check gauge.

Notes

I Work gauge swatch in sc only to determine proper gauge.

2 When working the wave pat rows in colors B, C and D, beg and end each row with either 2 sc or 2 tr.

3 Scarf is made lengthwise and from center to sides, first working side 1, then turning piece to work in opposite side of foundation row, side 2.

SCARF – SIDE I
Beg at center with B, ch 322.

Row 1 (RS) Working into single (top) loop of foundation ch only, 1 sc in 2nd ch from hook, *1 sc in next ch, ch 1, skip 1 ch, 1 hdc in next ch, ch 1, skip 1 ch, 1 dc in next ch, [ch 1, skip 1 ch, 1 tr in next ch] twice, ch 1, skip 1 ch, 1 dc in next ch, ch 1, skip 1 ch, 1 hdc in next ch, ch 1, skip 1 ch, 1 sc in next ch, ch 1, skip 1 ch; rep from *, end last rep by working 2 sc in each of last 2 ch (do not skip 1 ch between the 2 sc), pull A through last 2 lps on hook, ch 1, turn. There are 321 sts and 20 wave pat reps.

Row 2 With A, 1 sc in each ch-sp and st across, ch 1, turn.

Row 3 With A, 1 sc in each sc across, drawing C through last 2 lps on hook, ch 1, turn.

Row 4 With C, ch 4 (counts as first tr), *1 tr in next st, ch 1, skip 1 st, 1 dc in next st, ch 1, skip 1 st, 1 hdc in next st, [ch 1, skip 1 st, 1 sc in next st] twice, ch 1, skip 1 st, 1 hdc in next st, ch 1, skip 1 st, 1 dc in next st, ch 1, skip 1 st, 1 tr in next st, ch 1, skip 1 st; rep from *, end last rep by working 2 tr in each of last 2 sts (do not skip 1 ch between the 2 tr), turn.

Row 5 Rep row 4.

Rows 6 and 7 Rep rows 2 and 3.

Rows 8 and 9 With B, ch 1, rep row 1, only working into sts instead of foundation ch, pull A through last 2 lps on hook, ch 1, turn.

Rows 10 and 11 Rep rows 2 and 3.

Rows 12 and 13 With D, rep rows 4 and 5, pull A through last 2 lps on hook, ch 1, turn.

Rows 14 and 15 Rep rows 2 and 3. Fasten off.

With RS of piece facing and working along opposite side of foundation ch (into the unworked lps), work rows 1-15 as for side 1 with these color exceptions: for rows 4 and 5 use D instead of C and for rows 12 and 13 use C instead of D.

For short edges of scarf, from RS join A with a sl st.

Row I (RS) Ch 1, work 39 sc evenly along end of scarf, ch 1, turn.

Row 2 Work 1 sc in each sc across. Fasten off.

A series of openwork lengths of rectangles, dots and dashes are joined together in this breezy scarf design. Reminiscent of 1960's wind chimes, it's designed by Anna Mishka.

FINISHED MEASUREMENTS
■ Approx 5½"/14cm wide x 50"/127cm long

MATERIALS
■ 1 1¾oz/50g skein (each approx 175yd/158m) of Koigu Wool Design *Premium 2-ply Merino* (wool) each of #1013 lilac (A), #2339 lime (B), #2343 lt green (C), #1005 med blue (D), #2151 pale green (E) #2323 pale blue (F) and #2300 lt blue (G) (2)
■ Size D/3 (3mm) crochet hook *or size to obtain gauge*

GAUGE
28 sc and 28 rows to 4"/10cm over sc pat st using size D/3 (3mm) hook.
Take time to check gauge.

Notes
1 The 7 colors are used in this design in a random combination of your choice. Just be sure that colors are alternated so that the same colors are not placed next to each other.
2 At completion of motifs, one more set of tails will be worked on 6 motifs to attach the discs and join the motifs to scarf points.

RECTANGLE MOTIF WITH TAIL
(Make 10 of each of 6 colors, 9 of the 7th color for a total of 69.)
Ch 14.
Row 1 (WS) Work 1 hdc in 3rd ch from hook, 1 hdc in each ch to end—12 hdc. Ch 11 (for tail), turn.
Row 2 Work 1 sc in 2nd ch from hook, 1 sc in each of next 9 ch, 1 hdc in each of next 12 hdc, turn.
Row 3 Ch 2, 1 hdc in first 10 hdc, [yo and draw up a lp in next hdc] twice, yo and draw through all 5 lps on hook for hdc2tog, turn, leaving rem sts unworked for tail.
Row 4 Ch 2, hdc2tog over first 2 sts, 1 hdc in next 7 hdc, hdc2tog over last 2 sts. Fasten off.

DISC
(Make 2 of each color for a total of 12.)
Ch 2.
Rnd 1 Work 8 sc in 2nd ch from hook, join with sl st to first sc. Cont to work in rnds.
Rnd 2 Ch 1, work 2 sc in each sc around—16 sc. Join with sl st to first sc.
Rnd 3 Ch 1, 2 sc in first sc, *1 sc in next sc, 2 sc in next sc; rep from * to last sc, 1 sc in last sc—24 sc. Join with sl st to first sc.
Rnd 4 Ch 1, 1 sc in first sc, *2 sc in next sc, 1 sc in each of next 2 sc; rep from * to last 2 sc, 2 sc in next sc, 1 sc in last sc—32 sc. Join with sl st to first sc.
Rnd 5 Ch 1, 2 sc in first sc, *1 sc in each

of next 3 sc, 2 sc in next sc; rep from * to last 3 sc, 1 sc in each of last 3 sc—40 sc. Join with sl st to first sc. Fasten off.

FINISHING

For 6 of the rectangle motifs, make one additional tail at opposite end of the rectangle as foll: join with sl st in matching color at center of rectangles, and ch 11, sc in 2nd ch from hook and in each ch. Fasten off. These 6 motifs with 2 tails will form one end of scarf, the end without tails will be at the center of the scarf. Foll photo, join motifs tog at points in the 6 alternating strips of [11 motifs, 12 motifs] 3 times. Join discs, alternating colors, to tail ends at each end of scarf.

■■■□

A vintage-inspired scarf—featuring delicate flowers in an allover openwork pattern—evokes fond memories of a by-gone era. Designed by Anna Mishka, stitch it up in a lightweight wool yarn.

Note
Read instructions completely before beg to crochet. Motifs are made partially and then joined in description that follows.

Motif I
(Make 1 first, then make further motifs as joining motifs.)
With A, ch 6. Join with sl st to first ch to form ring.
Rnd I Ch 1, work 12 sc in ring, join with sl st to first sc. Fasten off.

Rnd 2 Join B with a sl st in any sc, ch 1, 1 sc in same sc as sl st joining, *ch 7, 1 sc in next sc; rep from * 10 times more, ch 7, join with sl st to first sc. Fasten off

Motif 2
(make a total of 39) Make 1 first. Then make further motifs as joining motifs and join foll motif layout.
Work as for motif 1, substituting color B for color A and color A for color B.

Side motif I
(make 26 and work as previous motifs.)
With A, ch 6. Join with sl st to first ch to form ring.
Rnd I Ch 1, work 12 sc in ring, join with sl st to first sc. Fasten off.
Rnd 2 Join B with a sl st in any sc, ch 1, 1 sc in same sc as sl st joining, *ch 7, 1 sc in next sc; rep from * 8 times more, 1 sc in each of last 2 sc, join with sl st to first sc. Fasten off.

Side motif 2
(make 24 and work as previous motifs.)
Work as for side motif 1, substituting color B for color A and color A for color B.

Corner motif I
(make 2 and work as previous motifs.)
With A, ch 6. Join with sl st in first ch to form ring.
Rnd I Ch 1, work 12 sc in ring, join with a sl st to first sc. Fasten off.
Rnd 2 Join B with a sl st to any sc, ch 1, 1 sc in same sc as sl st joining, *ch 7, 1 sc in

next sc; rep from * 5 times more, 1 sc in each of next 2 sc, ch 2, 1 sc in each of last 3 sc, join with sl st to first sc. Fasten off.

Corner motif 2

(make 2 and work as previous motifs.)
Work as for corner motif 1, substituting color B for color A and color A for color B.

Joining 2 motifs

After completion of one motif, join 2 motifs along one side as foll:
Using appropriate color, ch 6. Join with sl st to form ring.

Rnd 1 Ch 1, work 12 sc in ring, join with sl st to first sc. Fasten off.

Joining rnd 2 With appropriate color, join with a sl st in any sc, ch 1, 1 sc in same sc as sl st joining, [ch 3, sl st to 4th ch of adjoining motif, ch 3, 1 sc in next sc] 3 times, [ch 7, 1 sc in next sc] 8 times, ch 7, join with sl st to first sc. Fasten off.

Joining 3 motifs

Using appropriate color, ch 6, join with sl st to form ring.

Rnd 1 Ch 1, work 12 sc in ring, join with sl st to first sc. Fasten off.

Joining rnd 2 With appropriate color, join with a sl st in any sc, ch 1, 1 sc in same sc as sl st joining, [ch 3, sl st to 4th ch of first adjoining motif, ch 3, 1 sc in next sc] 3 times, [ch 3, sl st to 4th ch of 2nd adjoining motif, ch 3, 1 sc in next sc] 3 times, [ch 7, 1 sc in next sc] 5 times, ch 7, join with sl st to first sc. Fasten off.

Joining 4 motifs

Work as for previous joinings up to rnd 2.
Joining rnd 2 With appropriate color, join with a sl st in any sc, ch 1, 1 sc in same sc as sl st joining, [ch 3, sl st to 4th ch of first adjoining motif, ch 3, 1 sc in next sc] 3 times, [ch 3, sl st to 4th ch of 2nd adjoining motif, ch 3, 1 sc in next sc] 3 times, [ch 3, sl st to 4th ch of third adjoining motif, ch 3, 1 sc in next sc] 3 times, [ch 7, 1 sc in next sc] twice, ch 7, join with sl st to first sc. Fasten off.

MOTIF LAYOUT

Motif Key

⊠ Motif 1

◯ Motif 2

⊠ Corner motif 1

◉ Corner motif 2

◥ Side motif 1

◖ Side motif 2

Joining 5 motifs

Work as for previous joinings up to rnd 2.

Joining rnd 2 With appropriate color, join with a sl st in any sc, ch 1, 1 sc in same sc as sl st joining, [ch 3, sl st to 4th ch of first adjoining motif, ch 3, 1 sc in next sc] 3 times, [ch 3, sl st to th ch of 2nd adjoining motif, ch 3, 1 sc in next sc] 3 times, [ch 3, sl st to 4th ch of 3rd adjoining motif, ch 3, 1 sc in next sc] 3 times, [ch 3, sl st to 4th ch of 4th adjoining motif, ch 3, 1 sc in next sc] twice, ch 3, sl st to 4th ch of 4th adjoining motif, ch 3, join with sl st to first sc. Fasten off.

Cont to join motifs in this way, foll motif layout diagram for positions of motifs.

EDGING

Join A with sl st to any corner ch-2 sp, ch 1, work 3 sc in corner sp, sc in next sc, ch 3, sl st in top of last sc for *picot*, 1 sc in each of next 3 sc, 1 sc in next ch-3 sp, work picot, 2 more sc in same ch-3 sp; then cont in this way around, working picot in every 4th st and 1 sc in each sc and 3 sc in each ch-3 sp and 3 sc in each corner. Fasten off.

A plush mohair is worked in two colors to produce this stylish granny square scarf. Designed by Diane Zangl, this easy-to-crochet snowflake motif is a cinch to re-create.

FINISHED MEASUREMENTS
■ Approx 5½"/14cm wide x 55"/139.5cm long

MATERIALS
■ 2 1¾oz/50g balls (each approx 108yd/100m) of Naturally/SR Kertzer *Woodland 12 Ply* (mohair/acrylic/nylon/polyester) each in #06 pink (MC) and #07 red (CC) 🔢
■ Size F/5 (4mm) crochet hook *or size to obtain gauge.*

GAUGE
1 medallion is 5½"/14cm square.
Take time to check gauge.

MEDALLION
Make 10
With CC, ch 8. Join with sl st to first ch to form ring.
Rnd 1 Ch 6, [1 dc, ch 3] 7 times into ring, join MC with sl st to 4th ch of ch-6.
Rnd 2 With MC, (ch 2, 3 dc, ch 2) in first sp, *4 dc, ch 2 in next sp; rep from * around, join CC with sl st to top of ch-2.
Rnd 3 With CC, (ch 3, 5 dc, ch 3) in first sp, *(6 dc, ch 1) in next sp, (6 dc, ch 3) in

foll sp; rep from * twice, (6 dc, ch 1) in last sp, join MC with sl st to top of ch-3.
Rnd 4 With MC, ch 3, 1 sc between 3rd and 4th dc of next group, *ch 3, (2 dc, ch 3, 2dc) in next ch-3 sp at corner, ch 3, 1 sc between 3rd and 4th dc of next group, ch 3, 1 sc in ch-1 sp, 1 sc between 3rd and 4th dc of next group; rep from * twice, end ch 3, (2 dc, ch 3, 2dc) in last ch-3 sp at corner, ch 3, 1 sc between 3rd and 4th dc of last group, ch 3, sl st in first ch at beg of rnd.
Rnd 5 Work 1 sc between each dc, 4 sc in each corner sp and 3 sc in each ch-3 sp around, join with sl st.
Rnd 6 *Ch 4, skip 1 sc, sl st in next sc; rep from * around. Fasten off.

JOIN MEDALLIONS
Join MC to corner loop of one square, ch 2, sl st in corner loop of 2nd square, *ch 2, sl st in next loop of opposite square; rep from * until all loops along 1 side have been joined. Fasten off. Join rem squares in same way.

EDGING
Join MC in any ch-4 loop. Work 2 sc in each ch-4 loop around entire scarf, working 3 sc in each corner loop.

FINISHING
Brush lightly to give mohair a fur effect as in photo.

MULTICOLOR MESH SCARF

In living color

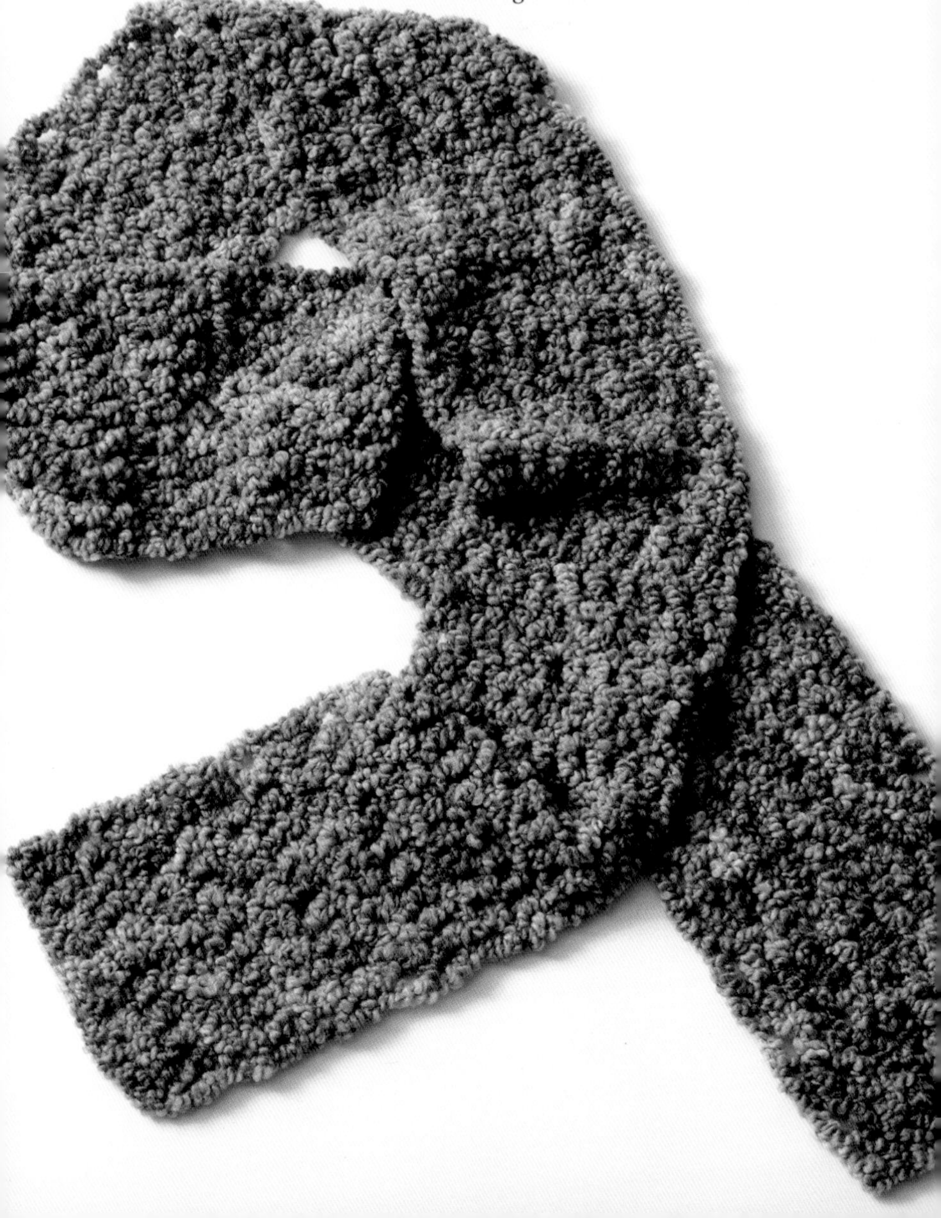

A perfect project for beginners, this easy-to-crochet scarf—designed by Norah Gaughan—stitches up in a flash. The nubby yarn, along with the brilliant multi-color shading, adds maximum interest.

KNITTED MEASUREMENTS
Approx 6½"/16.5cm x 78"/198 cm

MATERIALS
2 3½oz/100g balls (each approx 93yd/86m) of Artful Yarns/JCA Inc *Circus* (wool/acrylic) in 712 blue/orange multi (6)
Size N/15 (10mm) crochet hook *or size to obtain gauge*

GAUGE
7 dc and 4 rows to 4"/10cm over dc pat st using size N/15 (10mm) hook
Take time to check gauge.

Note (on gauge) When an extra bulky weight of yarn is used in combination with this very large hook size, it is not recommended to change hook sizes to fit the stated gauge. Therefore, try to work the gauge swatch with a looser or tighter tension to achieve the look of the fabric in this style.

Note (on ends) You may want to crochet over the ends while working to avoid weaving in later.

SCARF
Chain 13.

Row 1 Work 1 dc in 3rd ch from hook and in each ch to end—11 dc, turn.

Row 2 Ch 2 (counts as 1 dc), work 1 dc in next dc and in each dc across, ending 1 dc in t-ch, turn.

Rep row 2 for dc pat st until piece measures approx 78"/198cm. Fasten off.

RESOURCES

*Write to the yarn
companies listed below for
purchasing and mail-order
information.*

ANNY BLATT
7796 Boardwalk
Brighton, MI 48116

ARTFUL YARNS
distributed by
JCA

BERROCCO, INC.
P.O. Box 367
Uxbridge, MA 01569

BROWN SHEEP CO.
100662 County Road 16
Mitchell, NE 69357

CLASSIC ELITE YARNS
300A Jackson Street
Lowell, MA 01852

DALE OF NORWAY
N16 W23390 Stoneridge
Drive, Suite A
Waukesha, WI 53188

FIESTA YARNS
206 Frontage Road Drive,
Rio Rancho, NM 87124

FILATURA DI CROSA
distributed by
Tahki•Stacy Charles, Inc.

GGH
distributed by
Muench Yarns

JAMIESONS
distributed by
Unicorn Books & Crafts

JCA
35 Scales Lane
Townsend, MA 01469

KNIT ONE CROCHET TOO
7 Commons Ave., Suite 311
Windham, ME 04062

KOIGU WOOL DESIGNS
RR#1
Williamsford, ON N0H 2V0

LBUSA
PO Box 217
Colorado Springs, CO 80903

LE FIBRE NOBILI
distributed by
Plymouth Yarn

LION BRAND YARN CO.
34 West 15th Street
New York, NY 10011

MUENCH YARNS
285 Bel Marin Keys Blvd.
Unit J
Novato, CA 94949

NATURALLY
distributed by
S. R. Kertzer, Ltd.

PATON® YARNS
PO Box 40
Listowel, ON N4W3H3
Canada

PLYMOUTH YARN
PO Box 28
Bristol, PA 19007

ROWAN YARNS
4 Townsend West, Unit 8
Nashua, NH 03063

S. R. KERTZER LTD.
105 A Winges Road
Woodbridge, ON L4L 6C2
Canada

SESIA
distributed by
LBUSA

**SKACEL COLLECTION,
INC.**
PO Box 88110
Seattle, WA 98138-2110

**TAHKI•STACY CHARLES,
INC.**
8000 Cooper Ave.
Brooklyn, NY 11222

TRENDSETTER YARNS
16742 Stagg Street
Suite 104
Van Nuys, CA 91406

UNIQUE KOLOURS
1428 Oak Lane
Downingtown, PA 19335

**UNICORN BOOKS &
CRAFTS**
1338 Ross Street
Petaluma, CA 94954

ZITRON
distributed by Skacel
Collection

*Write to US resources for
mail-order availability
of yarns not listed.*

BERROCO, INC.
distributed by
S. R. Kertzer, Ltd.

CLASSIC ELITE YARNS
distributed by
S. R. Kertzer, Ltd.

CLECKHEATON
distributed by
Diamond Yarn

DIAMOND YARN
9697 St. Laurent
Montreal, PQ H3L 2N1
and
155 Martin Ross, Unit #3
Toronto, ON M3J 2L9

**LES FILS MUENCH,
CANADA**
5640 rue Valcourt
Brossard, PQ J4W 1C5

MUENCH YARNS, INC.
distributed by
Les Fils Muench, Canada

NATURALLY
distributed by
S. R. Kertzer, Ltd.

PATONS ®
PO Box 40
Listowel, ON N4W 3H3

ROWAN
distributed by
Diamond Yarn

S. R. KERTZER, LTD.
105A Winges Rd.
Woodbridge, ON L4L 6C2

*Not all yarns used in this
book are available in
the UK. For yarns not
available, make a
comparable substitute or
contact the US manufacturer
for purchasing and
mail-order information.*

ROWAN YARNS
Green Lane Mill
Holmfirth
West Yorks HD7 1RW
Tel: 01484-681881

SILKSTONE
12 Market Place
Cockermouth
Cumbria, CA13 9NQ
Tel: 01900-821052

**THOMAS RAMSDEN
GROUP**
Netherfield Road
Guiseley
West Yorks LS20 9PD
Tel: 01943-872264

VOGUE KNITTING CROCHETED SCARVES

Editorial Director
TRISHA MALCOLM

Yarn Editor
VERONICA MANNO

Art Director
CHI LING MOY

Production Manager
DAVID JOINNIDES

Executive Editor
CARLA S. SCOTT

Photography
QUENET STUDIOS

Book Manager
MICHELLE LO

Photo Stylist
LAURA MAFFEO

Graphic Designer
CAROLINE WONG

Instructions Editor
MARI LYNN PATRICK

President, Sixth&Spring Books
ART JOINNIDES

LOOK FOR THESE OTHER TITLES IN THE *VOGUE KNITTING ON THE GO!* SERIES...

BABY BLANKETS

BABY BLANKETS TWO

BABY GIFTS

BABY KNITS

BAGS & BACKPACKS

BEGINNER BASICS

CAPS & HATS

CAPS & HATS TWO

CHUNKY KNITS

KIDS KNITS

MITTENS & GLOVES

PILLOWS

SCARVES

SCARVES TWO

SOCKS

SOCKS TWO

TEEN KNITS

TODDLER KNITS

VESTS

VINTAGE KNITS

WEEKEND KNITS